Listening to the Animals

UNCONDITIONAL LOVE

EDITED BY PHYLLIS HOBE

A GUIDEPOSTS BOOK

ACKNOWLEDGMENTS

Every attempt has been made to credit the sources of copyrighted material used in this book. If any such acknowledgment has been inadvertently omitted or miscredited, receipt of such information would be appreciated.

All material that originally appeared in *Guideposts* magazine, *Angels on Earth* or *Daily Guideposts* is reprinted with permission. Copyright © 1995, 1996, 1997.

"Everybody Needs a Bubba," by Diane M. Ciarloni, is used by permission of the author.

"The Laska Chronicles," by Julie Ann Mock, is from *Circles of Compassion,* edited by Elaine Sichel. Copyright © 1995, 1998 Elaine Sichel. Published by Voice & Vision Publishing.

"The Dog Who Showed Me What Love Is," by Debbie Burkitt, and "A Parrot Taught Me Her Song," by Ronald L. Harmon, are from *Angel Animals,* by Allen and Linda Anderson. Copyright © William Allen Anderson and Linda C. Anderson, 1999. Published by The Penguin Group.

"Cliffie," by Crystal Ward Kent, is used by permission of the author.

"The Short Stranger," by Gina Romsdahl, is used by permission of the author.

"Suki, the Reject," by Diana Pullein-Thompson, is from *Best-Loved Dog Stories,* edited by Vanessa Mitchell. Copyright © 1998 by Michael O'Mara Books Limited. Published by The Reader's Digest Association, Inc.

"Real Cowboys Don't Cry," by Lenton McClendon, is used by permission of the author.

"Bunny Rab," by Anne Watkins, is used by permission of the author.

"Just the Same," by Katherine L. Hall, is used by permission of the author.

"A Special Greeting," by Edward Grinnan, appeared in *Daily Guideposts 1996.*

"Gus, the Big White Dog," by Brenda Randolph, is used by permission of the author.

"Waiting for Friendship," by Phyllis Hobe appeared in *Daily Guideposts 1995.*

"The Lost Dog" and "Another Daisy" are from *Tears & Laughter,* by Gene Hill. Copyright © 1981 by Gene A. Hill. Published by Countrysport Press.

"Friends" is from *Animal Angels,* by Stephanie Laland. Copyright © 1997 by Stephanie Laland. Published by Guideposts.

"Griz" and "A Distant Cry" are from *The Compassion of Animals,* by Kristin von Kreisler. Copyright © 1997 by Kristin von Kreisler. Published by Prima Publishing.

"Sam and Sadie," by Sharon Surber, and "Rusty," by Karen Derrico, are from *Unforgettable Mutts,* by Karen Derrico. Copyright © 1999 by Karen Derrico. Published by NewSage Press.

"My Angel With Fur," by Pamela Santi Meunier, and "Ain't Nothing Better Than a Coonhound," by Joan Embree, are from *Angels With Fur,* by Pamela Santi Meunier. Copyright © 2000 by Pamela Santi Meunier. Published by Galactica Press.

(continued on page 208)

Designed by SMS Typography
Illustrations by Michelle Lester
Jacket designed by Dennis Arnold
Printed in the United States of America

Contents

THE HEART KNOWS BEST

A Generous Spirit

TRUSTING OTHERS

Watching Out for Us

Introduction

$\mathcal{L}$ike everyone else, I have days when I can't seem to do anything right. I make mistakes, I forget obligations, my decisions are faulty and I let people down—all with the best of intentions. At the end of such a day I feel quite unlovable, and sometimes even my dearest friends and family members are a little put out with me. But not my animals.

No matter how disastrous the day or how many mistakes I have made, my animals let me know they love me. If I'm coming home to them, they greet me as if I'm someone special. If I've been with them all day and they see my distress, they stay very close. They seem to want to remind me that, mistakes and all, I'm worth loving. I can't help but feel that they're telling me that this is the way God loves all of us.

UNCONDITIONAL LOVE, one of the books in Guideposts' exclusive *LISTENING TO THE ANIMALS* series, brings you true stories about the special love between animals and people. And you will rejoice in the many ways our animal friends help us to find ways in which we, too, can be a blessing to others.

In *Always Patient,* our first chapter, Diane Ciarloni writes about her first cat, Bubba, who taught her to make room in her heart for a creature she thought she didn't like—and then fell in love with! "Cliffie," by Crystal Ward Kent, is a touching story about a delightful dog whose only fault was that he was very big, and a young man who really didn't care about size.

The stories in *The Heart Knows Best* illustrate those times when our feelings have to overrule our common sense. In "Just the Same," Katherine Hall writes about the sick puppy she was about to give up, but didn't. And Gene Hill's story, "The Lost Dog," will speak to those who still hope that a beloved animal will someday come home.

In *A Generous Spirit,* we meet Griz, a huge bear recovering in a rehabilitation center, who formed a most unusual friendship with a needy little kitten. Kathy Beth MacDonald's story, "Memories," takes us into a nursing home along with a little mixed-breed dog named Heather who brings love and companionship to lonely people.

Trusting Others introduces us to both animals and people who didn't always get the right start in life. In Anne Watkins story, "Nobody's Bird," a woman who is warned to avoid a disagreeable parrot finds an unexpected and delightful friendship. "Side By Side," Sissy Burggraf's touching story about two devoted horses who finally have a chance for a decent life, will linger in your mind.

The stories in *Watching Out for Us* remind us that, while we may consider ourselves the caretakers of our animals, they often look after us. In "The First Cat," Renie Szilak Burghardt recalls some years of her childhood when she and her family— and her beloved cat—were refugees during World War II. In "Ode to Bob Dog," Brenda Randolph remembers, with great affection, the devoted, but rather difficult dog who was her father's best friend.

All of the true stories in UNCONDITIONAL LOVE make a point: when we love someone, or when someone loves us,

there are no strings attached. We may not be perfect, and neither may they, but that doesn't matter. We just love each other,
the way God loves each of us. That's something we can learn
from our animal friends.

PHYLLIS HOBE

UNCONDITIONAL LOVE

ALWAYS PATIENT

" . . . *the patient in spirit is better than*
the proud in spirit."

ECCLESIASTES 7:8, RSV

$\mathcal{S}$ome of the happiest moments in my life have been spent with my animals. It doesn't matter whether we play ball, go for a ride, visit friends or take long walks. Being together is what counts. I used to think I had to do something to win their love, because that's the way people often are. But my animals taught me that all I had to do was be me. How did they do that? By putting up with all my efforts to please them until I finally realized that I already had their love. It had been there all along.

Everybody Needs a Bubba

DIANE M. CIARLONI

A cat has nine lives and nine souls,
and it must also have nine guardian
angels watching over it. Which would explain
why the little fellow is so smug.

KAREN FIELDS-HUTTON

It was July, 1984, and I was trying to make sense of my garage. It was definitely not a fun project, and the stifling Texas heat and humidity increased the misery barometer significantly. The sweat running down my forehead and stinging my eyes made it difficult to believe there was any chance of bringing order from the chaos.

"Maybe I should have a garage sale," I muttered to myself. "I could probably make enough money to at least buy shelves for this place."

I was dragging another box across the concrete floor when my peripheral vision suddenly caught sight of a bright orange streak bending underneath a wheelbarrow.

"Hey!" I yelled. "What was that?" As soon as the words were out of my mouth, I began wondering why in the world a wheelbarrow was in the garage in the first place. No wonder there was no available space.

Nothing responded. I was only seconds away from making up my mind to ignore whatever it was when I saw it again. This time, if possible, it was even faster—a flash of orange shot through with white. It was so fast that it seemed to slither. Being near-phobic about snakes, I silently questioned whether or not the abhorrent things might come in an orange and white color scheme.

"Okay," I said. "I saw you. You moved. C'mon out." Nothing.

I was in no mood to play games, but I did need to find out what was darting around in my garage. Whatever it was, the slight movement underneath a pile of old blankets gave away its location. I tiptoed as quietly as possible, starting to bend at the waist as I made my way to the stack. Reaching the quilts, I leaned forward and grabbed a corner of the top blanket, yanking it back as quickly as possible. What I saw was a big-eyed, orange and white kitten. He stared at me, trapped, no doubt wondering what I intended to do. I picked him up and held him at arm's length, allowing him to dangle in mid-air.

"Look," I said, "this is a dog house. There are no cats here, and that's something I do not intend to change. I'm certain some uncaring soul dumped you in the woods. I'm sorry about that, but you're really not my problem."

I turned, still carrying the kitten, and marched across the expanse of concrete that separated my house from the woods in back. The dense forest belonged to the Corps of Engineers, and it offered a fertile dumping ground for unwanted animals. I put the kitten down at the juncture of concrete and woods, giving him a slight push on his skinny rear end. "Go," I said. "There are houses all around here. Check 'em out. You'll find somebody who'll want you." As skinny as he was, I couldn't help but wonder if he'd already used up one of those nine lives I'd always heard cats possessed. "Not my problem," I muttered again.

I didn't linger to find out which direction the kitten chose, but neither did it take long for me to find out. An orange and white blur moved with the speed of light around the edge of the garage door. I lost no time tracking him down and returning him, again, to the edge of the woods.

"Look," I said. "This is nothing personal, but I'm telling you I don't want a cat. Why? Well, because I don't *like* cats, and I know no self-respecting cat would want to live where he isn't liked." Somehow I felt I'd not made my point with the kitten. I leaned down closer to his face.

"I don't even know anything about cats," I said. "I wouldn't know if you didn't feel well. You'd be dead by the time I realized there was something wrong with you. This just isn't an arrangement that would work to anyone's benefit."

This time I pushed the kitten on the butt, turned and ran into the garage. I glanced over my shoulder, watching him as he stood there with a puzzled look on his face. Then, before he had a chance to run back to the garage, I jammed the button and watched as the door went down. The kitten was cut off from view.

I really felt bad about the situation, but I had two dogs and that was enough. They weren't accustomed to cats, and I certainly didn't want a bunch of fights. Besides, I'd never had a cat in my life. So many people told me they were independent, had nothing to do with you unless they wanted to, had no personalities and on down the long list of anti-cat characterizations. So much for that.

I looked around at the garage, still piled high with, well, with mostly junk. Somehow my heart had gone out of the project. I wouldn't be able to put my car away if I elected to postpone finishing the odious task but, really, would it hurt it to be out one night? I made up my mind. I'd finish tomorrow. I just needed to move one box away from the door.

I walked to the door, bent down and heard a faint meow. Then I saw a tiny orange paw with a white freckle reach underneath the door at the exact spot where the weather stripping was missing. I sighed. "Okay. Fine. But nothing permanent." As I mumbled underneath my breath, I jabbed at the button to raise the door. I looked down and there sat the kitten, big eyes glowing and something vaguely resembling a smile on his face. He scampered into the garage. I snagged him as he was about to tear past me.

Again holding the kitten in front of me with his back legs dangling, I conducted a brief monologue with him. "Listen, I said no cats and I meant it. You can stay here one, maybe three, days at the most. I'll feed you but you're going somewhere else. I'll help you find a permanent home since you can't seem to do it on your own." The kitten never blinked. I'm convinced he knew he was here to stay and, somewhere deep down, I did, too.

I carried the waif into the house, allowing the two dogs to run up and begin sniffing. Their instincts kicked in and told them this was nothing more than a defenseless baby. Their curiosity was satisfied quickly.

I opened the refrigerator and took out milk. Everyone, even I, knows kittens like milk. "Hope you don't mind non-fat," I said without turning around. At a complete loss regarding any additional feline dietary needs, I pulled out a piece of ham and tore it into small pieces, dropping it into the milk. I later learned this wasn't exactly the way to do things but it didn't seem to bother the kitten.

We were into the fourth day. I looked at the kitten and knew I couldn't continue referring to him as "the kitten." He needed a name. I looked around. I'd moved to Texas from California and it didn't take me long to realize every household boasted at least one Bubba. I scooped the purring kitten off my lap and held him up, eye-to-eye and nose-to-nose with me. "That's it," I said to him. "You're Bubba."

The relationship that developed between me, Bubba and the dogs was incredible. Once he knew he was going to stay with us forever, Bubba marched into our lives and took over. Before he was named, it was as if he stood on the outskirts with just the tip of one paw peeking into our hearts. Not anymore.

My cousin, Barbara, lived 300 miles away in Houston. She'd been a cat person all her life and she became my guru. My phone bills grew to epic proportions.

"Barb," I said one evening, not even waiting for her to complete her hello. "Is it usual for a cat to eat mayonnaise?"

"Where's the mayonnaise?" she asked. Strange question, I thought.

"On the kitchen counter," I replied.

"And where's Bubba?" she queried.

"On the kitchen counter," I answered.

"Well, under those conditions I suppose it's normal for the cat to eat whatever he finds up there, provided he likes it." She sighed. "Your cat has no manners," she added.

"Barbara," I said during another long-distance session, "Bubba refuses to drink from a bowl."

"How does he drink?" she asked.

"Well, he has two ways. His favorite is to have me turn on the faucet in either the tub or kitchen sink. Then he gets up there, turns his head just right, and drinks from the stream."

"And the other way?" she asked. I could have sworn I heard just a tinge of something in her voice. Sarcasm?

"Well, it's not his favorite method but, if he has no choice, he'll sit next to the bowl, pick up the water in one paw, bring the paw to his mouth and drink from it."

"Drink from the paw?"

"Yes." I waited for a response. Nothing.

"Hello? Barb?"

I called her very early one morning. "Barb, I got up during the night to go to the bathroom. I turned on the water in the sink and Bubba was in there sleeping!"

I called her three and four times a week with cat questions. For my birthday she mailed me a huge cat encyclopedia. That was a bad choice. I know she thought she was doing something wonderful but, as I thumbed through the giant tome, I felt the same as I had all those years ago in Psych 101. I was convinced I suffered from every mental dementia on the page, and now I was convinced Bubba was afflicted with every physical scourge listed. I was miserable, and could hardly take my eyes off the growing kitten.

Bubba was less than two years old when he used another of his lives. Seemingly overnight he became deathly ill. I rushed him to the vet, and was told he had a life-threatening urinary tract infection. I stayed with him while he was put into a kennel and hooked up to IVs. His eyes stayed glued to my face, and it broke my heart to leave him. He was at the clinic 10 days, and I visited him twice each day. Some days I took Smudge, my Cavalier Spaniel, who was very attached to the orange tabby.

Finally, he was released with a permanently damaged kidney and placed on special—and very expensive—food. The cost didn't matter. A household without a Bubba just hadn't been the same.

Bubba has always been unique. Certainly proof of that quality is the manner in which he laid down his third life.

It was January and we were experiencing one of our brief cold snaps. The day before I'd gone to the grocery to buy all the ingredients for homemade soup. I'm one of those people who feels it's ridiculous to go through all that trouble for one pitiful little pot. Instead, I cook one and maybe even two caldron-like containers.

All the vegetables were cut and peeled the night before. The hamburger was browned. I threw everything into the pot early that morning and let it begin doing its thing. I was in the kitchen stirring and tasting the bubbling concoction after four hours of cooking. I have never determined what, if anything, possessed him, but Bubba came streaking from nowhere and leaped on to the stove. At least, that's what he intended. Instead, he leaped too high and too wide and came down smack into the boiling soup. I was horrified, even before he began screaming.

Without thinking, I plunged both my bare arms into the soup and grabbed Bubba underneath his front legs. I remember, even now, a horrible burning sensation but it wasn't enough to make me let go of him. There was also a disgusting stench, and hair was falling off of him as I pulled him out.

Holding the soup-soaked, struggling cat against my chest, I reached with one hand to turn on the cold water in the sink. I put Bubba underneath the stream. Holding him there, I stretched as far as I could and managed to open the refrigerator freezer and drag out the ice bin. I dumped it over him, rubbing the ice on him even though I knew it must be painful. I finally grabbed a couple of dish towels, wrapped him in them and drove to the vet clinic.

Bubba was tended to immediately. As soon as he was moderately comfortable, someone saw my red and blistered arms. I'd never noticed I was holding them away from my body. It hurt too much if they touched anything.

Oh, yes. Bubba lived. The vets said there was a good chance his hair would never grow back in some spots, but it grew back beautifully all over. They told me he might have a limp in one back leg. He was fine. The only permanent change in him was the way he would immediately exit the kitchen whenever he saw me remove a large pot from the cupboard. And me? Well, let's say I've never had quite the same taste for homemade soup as I once did.

Fortunately, not all of Bubba's escapades have been quite as dramatic as the soup. There was his first Christmas when I walked barefooted into the living room one evening. Suddenly, my foot made painful contact with something that crunched when I placed full weight on it. I turned on the light and saw a broken statue of Joseph. There, a bit farther away, were Mary and Baby Jesus. They were flanked by a shepherd and his flock. Then I looked under the Christmas tree at the Nativity scene. Bubba had cleared everybody out of the stable and appropriated it for his own napping spot. That was one Christmas when the term "no room at the inn" took on new meaning.

Bubba opened the way for many cats in my household. They seemed to troop through in a non-stop stream. I've had Kansas, Chico, Ginger, Highway, Doso, Jingle and Jonah. Some are still here. Each one has his own distinct personality, and each one is delightfully affectionate. They and all the dogs have gotten along without the slightest problem.

Bubba has laid down another life or two here and there, and he's beginning to tell me the time is probably not far off when he'll give up his last life and his last soul. The signs are all there. He has the gaunt look of an old, old cat. Now, when I turn on the faucet for him, he doesn't always see where to position his head. He gets wet, but I just reach for a towel and dry him when he gets down. And he's clinging closer to me, as if cramming in everything possible in the time we have left. Somehow, I can't help but think all nine of his guardian angels are with him and, somehow, I must trust in the wisdom they bring from God Himself—the very same God who made Bubba and Who gave him to me as my very first cat. That same God knows how it will feel to have a house without a Bubba.

The Laska Chronicles

JULIE ANN MOCK

The summer of 1993 wasn't much different from previous summers at the shelter: too many cats, too many kittens, and a constant struggle to accommodate and care for them all. Unlike most people, those of us who work or volunteer in animal shelters are never glad to see spring and summer come. There is an official mourning period in early March when we say goodbye to the low numbers of shelter residents typical during winter. A small population affords time for individualized care and the opportunity to take on creative projects to improve shelter life for the animals. Once spring arrives, so do kittens and a lot more cats.

Laska came to us during the first days of summer when the shelter was teeming with kittens and other adults. My volunteer job involves a variety of duties, including cleaning cages, giving medications, and helping with treatments in Sick Bay. Working with the cats in the Sick Bay provides an opportunity to get to know the ailing animals, but it leaves little chance to get to know the animals who are in the adoption area. Even so, I noticed Laska. She was a striking long-haired tortoise-shell patterned cat with white patches. She had been brought into the shelter by neighbors who said that her owners had moved and left her behind.

If I had known then what would eventually transpire, I would have paid better attention. But summers at the shelter are so busy time tends to rush by in a blur. I do remember observing Laska. She appeared to be a fairly large cat, very pretty and very proud, but rather reserved. I remember thinking to myself that she must have known she had been abandoned. She seemed hesitant to accept the modest comforts of shelter life and the attention of volunteers. I remember taking her out of her cage once or twice and holding her in my lap. She was polite and perhaps even purred a bit, but she still seemed detached.

It was when she stopped eating that I started to notice her more. She was put in Sick Bay with the hope that some fluids and extra attention would bring her around. When it comes to winning over frightened or depressed cats, we volunteers are a determined lot. We never say never. No matter how frightened or shy a cat may be initially, with enough patience and love we are almost always able to eventually elicit trusting purrs and nudges.

Neither the fluids nor the extra attention seemed to be getting the desired results with Laska though. She continued losing weight, and her food remained untouched. We pressed on though, certain that like so many others before her, she would respond.

It was around this time that I was scheduled to take ten days off from shelter duties to help with a fundraising event for our volunteer program. With little experience in putting on such an event, I became consumed with the task at hand. I'm ashamed to say that during my time away from the shelter, I never once thought about Laska.

When I returned to work though, I learned that her condition had deteriorated to the point where the shelter veterinarian was recommending euthanasia. Too weak to stand, and incontinent, Laska was a heartbreaking sight to see. With any other cat in such poor condition, I would have supported the decision that immediate euthanasia was the only choice and that the animal's suffering should be ended. But with Laska something was different. I couldn't stand the thought of losing her without ever knowing why she had stopped eating. There had to be a reason. Unless she was afflicted with a deadly disease, wasn't there *something* that could be done for her?

I remember taking her to the veterinarian in the bottom half of a plastic travel kennel. After years of witnessing first-hand the amazing speed, agility, and Houdini-like escape capabilities of most cats, it was a strange experience to have a cat in my car who wouldn't—indeed couldn't—go anywhere.

I brought Laska to work with me the next day to await the results of the blood panel. She was so near death that unless an answer could be found and some kind of treatment initiated, she would have to be euthanized. While I worked that morning, she lay silently in her carrier "bed," with officers and staff stopping by to offer a kind word or a pat on the head. When the time finally came to make the call to the veterinarian, I was nervous, yet resigned. The tests would tell us the right—though potentially heartbreaking—thing to do.

The blood work revealed only acute anemia, which was an obvious result of anorexia. The veterinarian prescribed an intensive course of syringe feeding, and some blood fortifying drugs and other medications, all of which might or might not save her. He wasn't willing to give up on her yet though, and neither was I.

My husband and I have an agreement which I grudgingly admit is fair: with all the time I spend at the shelter, our own very complete animal family, lots of travel, and a busy social schedule, I don't bring home foster animals. Exceptions to this have been rare, but when they have occurred they have been very temporary and their terms have been iron-clad. So, what to do? When all else failed, I opted for denial. These were my rationales: Though I wanted to believe otherwise, I was afraid Laska probably wasn't going to make it; we didn't have to worry about her disrupting our house, escaping or upsetting our own cats—she was too weak; and she would only stay with us until she started eating. The last item turned out to be the most laughable. Would I really have taken her back to the shelter where she had done so poorly—where her total food consumption could have fit on the head of a pin, and left room to spare?

The news that I was fostering Laska at my house was met with relief and expressions of joy and support from the other volunteers. When they hadn't seen her, they had feared she had been put down. Karen offered to help with her care if we had to go away, and Cindy offered the greatest of gifts—a potential home if Laska recovered. All of this assumed her survival.

Progress with Laska was slow, but it was steady. The veterinarian had warned that her recovery could take months and would require intensive care. At six pounds, she'd lost about half her body weight. One day as I combed some stray food from under her chin, a large patch of fur pulled loose! She was completely helpless. But she had only been with us a few days when it became clear that I was not to be her only nurse. Our shelter-adopted cat Melanie, a mother before she had come to us and been spayed, displayed all her maternal skills with Laska. She demanded to see her foundling, and with Laska's permission, was welcomed onto the rehabilitation team.

Hygiene is Melanie's specialty, and I'm certain that the once proud and immaculate Laska found comfort in her new friend's grooming services.

After ten days Laska started using a litter box placed near her bed. After three weeks of syringe feeding, she took her first bites of solid food. All the while, she was cheered on by friends who celebrated each small step as a major victory. These were my kind of people, who welcomed a phone call at ten at night to hear about Laska's first litter box trek, or who would stop by at feeding time just to watch Laska eat. Karen even brought warm baked chicken breasts to share with Laska.

When she started eating and moving around more easily, I brought her downstairs so she wouldn't be lonely. From her behavior at the shelter, I would not have expected Laska would be especially compatible with other cats, but she proved me wrong. Her manner was completely calm and non-threatening, even when my grumpiest male cat hissed in her face! As Laska's recovery progressed, she and Melanie took to conducting mutual grooming sessions. Afterwards they could often be seen sleeping together, sharing the same patch of morning sun.

Cindy's home was still available and Laska was quickly approaching the point at which she'd be ready for adoption. Meanwhile, my husband and I, who had no intention of keeping her, were fighting a losing battle against a cat with a story, and perhaps even a plan. Looking back, it seems as if it was inevitable. We were headed for the point of no return from day one. I was able to fool myself with the notion that the situation was temporary because Laska would have a home when she was ready. But Laska knew better. The cat who was reserved and elusive to so many made a brazen play for my husband

and charmed all our other animals into submission. Most importantly though, Laska *made* it. Hers was a story we loved being a part of, and once it was clear she had made it, we didn't want to let her go.

So Laska lives with us. We have had her for almost seven months now, in which time her coat has grown soft and shiny, she has gained two more pounds, and she has become a fairly good eater. In many ways she is still a mystery to us, bearing little resemblance to the gopher-hunting wonder the people who turned her in reported. She is sweet, has impeccable house manners, and gets along with everyone. Melanie, self-appointed feline social director of our household, would like to make a playmate out of Laska, but it remains to be seen if Laska, still recovering and not yet very active, will comply.

Laska likes to lick our hands and faces, purrs a lot, loves blankets, hates tile, and often sneaks into our bed at night to sleep between us. She gets fed whenever she wants, whatever she wants, wherever she wants (wouldn't you know, she prefers to eat on carpet)! She maintains a whole team of cheer-leaders ready to enjoy every chase of the tail and pretty pose.

All I want to know is, who writes these scripts? We can only laugh now about the unusual events which conspired to bring Laska to us. Whose design was it that a cat from outside the shelter's normal jurisdiction made her way to us, came very close to being euthanized but wasn't, wasn't given much chance of surviving but did, was taken into a foster home where foster animals weren't normally taken, and was adopted into that same home by people who had sworn that their animal family was large enough? My husband, always the pragmatist, is more than willing to blame at least the last three of these on me, but I know no mere mortal like myself could come close to creating such a scenario. One of my favorite songs asks, "Do you believe in fairy tales? Can love survive when all else fails?" You bet!

from CIRCLES OF COMPASSION

The Dog Who Showed Me What Love Is

DEBBIE BURKITT

A friend surprised me with the gift of a miniature pinscher dog. Although Brewster appeared healthy, it soon became obvious that he'd been abandoned and mistreated. When anyone tried to pet him, he'd duck and move away. When I called him, he'd run in the opposite direction. He'd hide under the furniture when he saw his collar and leash. But I knew there was hope for him when I noticed that he'd jump on the lap of and snuggle with anyone who sat on the couch. I could see that this dog had love in his heart. If only I knew what key would unlock it.

On the day my friend gave Brewster to me, I was feeling depressed. This little dog also seemed to be sad. He had no interest in my two cats or my friend's miniature pinscher. Brewster only wanted to snuggle and sleep with me that first night. The next morning he seemed even more sluggish. I had to carry him out of bed. The fleeting thought crossed my mind that being around me might be making Brewster more depressed than he had been. I wondered if he was empathizing with me to the point that he was relating to my sadness as if it were his own.

Later that day I silently asked God to help me understand the issue that was causing me to feel despondent. I asked for help in having a more balanced attitude about the situation. After my prayer, I felt my melancholy lifting and started feeling great. I walked around the house and found Brewster playing with my daughter and her father. They mentioned that the dog had perked up. Now my sense that perhaps Brewster was empathic became stronger.

During the next few months I asked God for help with my problems and I gained many new insights. I was feeling happier and more centered than I ever imagined being. However, as my burdens were becoming lighter, Brewster seemed to be carrying a heavier load. He became lethargic, difficult to wake up in the morning, and he rarely wanted to play for more than a moment. He didn't have much energy for his daily walks. To make matters worse, Brewster wasn't housebroken and often made messes on the carpet. Friends suggested that I didn't have to keep this dog. But Brewster reminded me of my own difficult times. I thought of people who had been "angels" and helped me along the way. I decided that I wouldn't abandon Brewster, a dog who had been let down by people far too often.

I asked God to help me understand how to be a friend to a dog with a bad case of the blues. I started thinking about stories I'd heard of animals who take on some of their human friends' karma, the effects of their past actions. I suddenly realized that the problem wasn't that Brewster was empathic. Instead, he'd made my burdens his own. No wonder he was so tired!

I called Brewster and sat down to have a heart-to-heart chat with him. I thanked him for his generous act of kindness. Then I told him he didn't have to carry the load of my pain and suffering anymore.

Within a few minutes of my talk with Brewster, I began to cry and feel anger welling up inside of me. I'd been feeling fine just moments before and didn't understand what could have triggered such an emotional response. Then I remembered. I'd just told Brewster that he didn't have to help me. In some spiritual way that I can't explain, he must have given my burdens back and they felt like bricks on my chest.

Since that day when I relieved Brewster of any responsibility he might have taken for my emotional well-being, the dog blossomed. He began getting up in the morning full of energy and ready to play. He wanted to be petted. He waited with anticipation for me to put on his collar and leash and take him for walks. I started having to run to keep up with him. He played ball like a happy puppy.

I think that by letting go of my burdens, Brewster somehow realized that he could release his own past traumas. He no longer acted like an abused and abandoned animal.

It humbles me to remember that I thought I was doing Brewster a service by keeping and loving him when he was lifeless and unhappy. But God enlisted this angel animal whose unconditional love helped me to move past a difficult issue and find true joy in my life.

from ANGEL ANIMALS

Cliffie

CRYSTAL WARD KENT

Why is one animal born into a home of pain and suffering, and another into a place of warmth and love? Surely that is one of the cruelest twists of fate—one puppy becomes a cherished companion, another, equally good, equally loveable, becomes the victim of cruel torment.

Many animals who live lives of suffering give up and die, or retreat into themselves. Even if rescued, the trauma to their psyche is so great that their spirit leaves although their body remains. A few, however, despite the horrors of their early years, triumph over the past. This is the story of one who did.

Cliffie was brought to the animal shelter by a young man who claimed the dog was a stray. The young Rottweiler was a horrible sight. He was hairless, underweight and covered with scabs from constant scratching. His suffering stemmed from rampant, untreated mange.

To shelter staff, something wasn't quite right with the young man's demeanor. He was fidgety and nervous, and eager to be gone. They asked for his driver's license, so they might contact him for more information, and he refused. Suddenly, he grabbed Cliffie by the scruff of the neck and dragged him out the door. Before they could stop him, the dog was thrown into the back of the man's truck. As the vehicle roared out of the driveway, staffers wrote down the license plate.

Police quickly tracked the truck down, and found that the young man was indeed Cliffie's owner—and abuser. The big dog had rarely been fed, slept outside, and was desperately in need of medical treatment. No one had ever petted or played with him. He was surrendered to the shelter, and Cliffie's second life began.

Underneath the layers of misery and pain, was a sweet, affectionate dog who loved to be cuddled and talked to. The veterinarian's evaluation showed that Cliffie was not the old dog he appeared to be, but a youngster, barely one-year in age. His mistreatment had caused him to stand in a cowed posture, giving the appearance of an elderly animal.

For three months, Cliffie lived at the shelter. Every two weeks he endured a complete submersion mite bath to rid him of his mange. Gradually, he began to gain weight and grow hair, and with constant gentle care and love, he began to stand tall. Another animal might have become depressed at having to undergo the constant medical treatment, and live at the shelter for so long, but Cliffie was different. Cliffie blossomed. As his energy returned, he revealed a playful, goofy side. He loved everyone, and would do anything to create a game or make people laugh.

Finally, Cliffie was ready for adoption, but now the shelter staff faced a new problem. Many people found Cliffie's looks intimidating. He was big and black and a Rottweiler—a breed frequently misunderstood. No one was taking the time to meet him and discover the loveable dog underneath.

One day, a young college student came in. He was tall and gangly and had a ready grin. As he talked with shelter staff, he had everyone laughing. He was also looking for a dog.

"He's a human Cliffie!" staffers whispered to each other. They just knew the two belonged together. Amazingly, as they showed the dogs, the fellow immediately asked for the big black Rottweiler. Cliffie's tail wagged and wagged. The pair went for a walk, and there was an instant and obvious bond.

One hurdle remained. The shelter staff were obligated to ensure that Cliffie went to a good, reliable home. They had to be certain the student was aware of all the obstacles and responsibilities he would face. The dog needed a home and had to be leashed on campus—not running loose. A Rottweiler running loose would cause special problems. The student would soon be graduating and taking a job—would there be time for Cliffie? The young man would then need an apartment, and not all landlords allowed dogs—or Rottweilers. He might even be asked to have special insurance.

The young man listened intently to all of their comments. He knew these were serious issues, but he really wanted the dog. He would work things out somehow. Would they hold Cliffie? They would. For two weeks, the young man visited Cliffie as often as he could. Finally, he showed up ready to adopt. He had a place to stay where Cliffie was allowed; he had a fiance who could dog sit when he worked, and the girl loved Cliffie, too.

Cliffie was deliriously happy. He knew he had a home at last. Fate had given his life another turn, but this time with wondrous results, matching a lonely dog with the one person perfect for him.

The Short Stranger

GINA ROMSDAHL

Little did I know that it was the first fortune cookie I ever had that would come true. It said, "A short stranger will soon enter your life."

I was living in a small, 26-foot trailer at the time. I opened the door one morning and there she was. If I had to guess, I would say she was some kind of dachshund/terrier mix. She had short, light brown hair, with a patch of white on her chest, and white front paws, like gloves. She was a small dog and couldn't have weighed more than fifteen pounds. She had a slight underbite that made her appear to be smiling when her teeth showed.

My dog Brandy bounded out of the trailer, as was his morning custom. Brandy was a beautiful collie/chow mix, with long, fox-colored hair, and was several times larger than our visitor. Despite the difference in size, Brandy and the visitor became fast friends. They spent the entire day playing and napping together, until I called Brandy in for the night. I assumed our new friend lived in the neighborhood and would find her way home.

The next morning when I opened the door I found her patiently waiting at the foot of the steps. She and Brandy greeted each other affectionately, and picked up their friendship where it had left off the day before. Not knowing her name, I began referring to her as "Shorty," in comparison to Brandy's large size.

I thought "Shorty's" owners might be concerned about her whereabouts, so I began inquiring of my neighbors to see if anyone recognized her or reported a missing dog. I was living in Baker, California, at the time. Baker is a small town with a population of approximately 300 people. It didn't take long to determine that "Shorty" was apparently homeless.

Baker is located in the Mojave desert, halfway between Las Vegas and Barstow. Unfortunately, it is not uncommon for people to abandon their companion animals in this desert wilderness. For some incomprehensible reason, they seem to think that domesticated animals will be able to fend for themselves "in the wild" simply because the area is largely unpopulated. The reality is that they are condemning their former pets to a slow death of starvation, dehydration and predation by truly wild animals.

As occasionally happens in the desert, a rising tide of water began flowing into the trailer park. Flash floods occur when the dry, sun-baked ground can't absorb rainwater fast enough, and it floods the surrounding areas. Our trailer would soon be underwater, and we had to move somewhere else for a night or two, until the water passed. I made the decision to take "Shorty" with us, and that night it became official: Shorty was now part of the family.

As Shorty realized that she was being accepted into the household, she quickly became extremely attached to me. She would follow me everywhere, even into the bathroom, and she became quite agitated if I was out of her sight. She seemed to view me as her protector, but she was wary of all other people.

It soon became apparent that someone had abused and

mistreated this small, gentle creature. If anyone raised his arms above a certain level, such as to open a cupboard door or answer the wall phone, Shorty would cower and hide, obviously in expectation of being hit. Voices raised in excitement and joy, much less anger, would terrify her. Someone had obviously tormented her cruelly in regard to food. It was obvious that she was hungry and very much wanted to eat, but she was afraid of being punished for it at the same time. She would hesitatingly approach the food bowl, inch by inch, and if anyone moved or came near her, she would instantly back away and tremble in fear. Although she was housebroken, she piddled frequently in fear, and I could not bring myself to reprimand her for it. She had suffered enough.

I suspect her tormentor might have been a man. Although she was wary of people in general, the deeper tones of mens' voices and the presence of masculine energy made her especially nervous.

In time, Shorty became more trusting of other people, and grew to seek out and enjoy affection, but it was a process that took many years. Her visible insecurities and fearful behaviors made many people uneasy. People expect dogs to be friendly and outgoing, and when a dog responds with inexplicable terror, most people are dumbfounded and just seem to find it easier to ignore the dog. Or they become apprehensive or insulted, which only serves to reinforce the dog's mistrust.

It took a lot of patience to see past Shorty's fears, and to allow her charms to show themselves, but they were there. I found her to be a delightful companion, and quite affectionate. She was the best snuggler I've ever known. At night, she slept next to me on the bed. She insisted on being under the blanket, but with her head exposed. She always had to feel my body next to her. If I wasn't close enough, she would scoot backwards until she was nestled next to me. This was sometimes uncomfortably warm on hot nights, but she wouldn't have it any other way.

After several weeks, she finally came to accept that she was entitled to eat and that no one would stop her. Her delight at mealtimes was abundantly evident. When she heard the can opener and rattle of food bowls, she would stand on her two hind legs and dance around me in joyous anticipation. I called her "my little dancing dog."

She enjoyed dancing on other occasions as well. I frequently listened to music, and my favorite songs would sometimes inspire me to dance around the room. Shorty would join me, twirling around on her rear legs. I would often pick her up and hold her while I danced. She didn't mind being jiggled and bounced, and she bobbed her head in time with the music. If I set her down, she would leap up for more, and I always obliged. She never tired of the game.

Shorty liked to have her belly rubbed, as many dogs do. She would lie on her back on the couch and bounce her back legs up and down, and beat her tail. The noise of this attention-getting scheme earned her the additional nickname of "Thumper."

Shorty and Brandy were best friends from the beginning and this never changed. Shorty also developed a close relationship with my cat Whiskey, a long-haired, orange tabby, who was barely more than a kitten when Shorty entered the picture. Whiskey, in her innocence, thought that Shorty needed to lighten up and have more fun, and she spared no effort in enticing Shorty to play. She would pounce on Shorty, trying to engage her in a game of cat and mouse. At first Shorty was perplexed, and couldn't be persuaded to do more than stare in wonder at this strange, furred being. Then Shorty would look at me in confusion, as if I could offer an explanation. Finally, perhaps in self-defense, Shorty learned to play the game. Whiskey would chase Shorty round and round in circles, and then Shorty would turn the tables on her, forcing Whiskey to become "the mouse." Shorty learned to enjoy the game and it became a frequent occurrence to see them taking turns chasing each other.

As Whiskey grew older, she developed a strong maternal instinct and Shorty became the object of her affection. She would lovingly groom and lick Shorty's head. A cat's tongue is rough, and Shorty didn't appreciate Whiskey's ministrations. Shorty would bare her teeth and growl at Whiskey to make her stop, but Whiskey knew Shorty too well. She knew that Shorty's effort to appear threatening was simply a laughable pretense, and would blithely continue licking away to her heart's content. Shorty would hang her ears in resignation, clearly not enjoying the attention, but tolerating it nonetheless.

Years passed, and we moved several times, finally ending up in San Francisco. As I was walking Shorty one day, she found a chicken bone that someone had discarded on the sidewalk, and began to eat it. Knowing that poultry bones can splinter and cause internal damage, I hollered at her to drop it. She ignored me and continued chewing. I knelt directly over her, tapping her on the head and yelled again for her to drop it. She continued to ignore me. Never had anything more than a raised voice, the barest suggestion of disapproval, been necessary to discipline her. This dog, who began her life in fear, who cowered and trembled at the slightest suggestion of anger, who was submissive even to kittens smaller than herself, was now ignoring outright yelling in her face and direct physical confrontation. I was so happy. As I pulled the bone out of her mouth with my fingers, I realized that she was finally healed.

Shorty was my constant companion for almost ten years. One day, just outside the edge of my driveway, Shorty was carelessly hit by a speeding car. The driver never even slowed down or looked back. I rushed to her and scooped her into my arms. She let out one shrill cry and died immediately. My heart was instantly broken. I'm glad she didn't suffer long, but I can't say the same for myself. Her death still brings tears to my eyes.

Exactly one month later, Brandy lay dying of grand mal epileptic seizures. As I waited for the veterinarian to come and administer the terminal injection, I sensed Shorty's presence. I had the distinct vision of Shorty dancing in excited anticipation of her reunion with her dear friend. It was the only consolation I had for losing my precious friends at nearly the same time. I knew that at least they would have each other. And I know that I, too, will join them in my turn. Many of life's mysteries and death's secrets are unknowable to us, but of this I am certain: love never dies and life goes on.

Suki, the Reject

DIANA PULLEIN-THOMPSON

It was a cold February day when I stared into a run full of miserable female dogs, all under one year old. These were society's young rejects with not a pedigree among them, animals picked up in the streets or found abandoned in house or shed and brought to a Midland city kennels. Now several had curled into tight, shivering balls of fur on the wet concrete floor. One opened an eye, looked at me as though to say, "No, you don't want me," and closed it again. I longed to take them all, but I had come to choose a calm, small one as a companion for our tall, thoroughbred, rough-coated collie, Angus, who was highly strung and hated being left alone.

"Surely these dogs are very ill?" I hazarded.

"It's grief," replied the kennel maid.

At the back, totally composed, stood Suki, a mixture, I suspect, of King Charles spaniel, working collie and, perhaps, long-haired dachshund. She was mainly black with beautiful reddish tan markings, which included a tan waistcoat, tan hoops above her appealing eyes, a tan muzzle, tan paws and undercarriage and lighter brown fluffier hair above her hocks which we later called her "plus fours." She met my eyes with an unwavering stare. And it was love at first sight. I paid four pounds fifty pence for Suki. She had only been in six, not the seven regulatory, days, but the official who gave me a receipt agreed to overlook the discrepancy.

I bought Suki a lead, clipped it on her mean collar which had Tipsy scratched on it, and we stepped out into the street without a backward glance. She walked to the station with utter composure, as though she had expected me to come to rescue her; she happily stepped into the train and halfway home decided to sit on my lap.

She entered our house with equal aplomb, and although mortified when I told her off for peeing on the breakfast-room carpet (from then on she was house-trained) she greeted Angus with controlled enthusiasm. I fed them in separate dishes. Suki gobbled her dinner and then approached Angus who, chivalrous to females but aggressive to his own sex, stepped back so she could gobble up his too. "No," I said. "No, no!" and Suki's intense desire to please ensured she never took her companion's food again.

Two days later Suki came on heat, which meant she must be about six months old. The vet said I should give her more time to settle down, before bringing her in for her routine vaccinations, but within twenty-four hours he saw her anyway, because she developed a runny nose, a distressing cough and a temperature of 105 degrees Fahrenheit. She had caught distemper, a would-be killer, which might leave her with St. Vitus's dance or epilepsy. Was it worth going on? the vet asked. His bills would be far higher than the four pounds fifty I had paid for this bedraggled little stray. Then my thoughts went back to Barney, whom my mother had nursed through distemper, a lovable black spaniel, who suffered occasionally from fits, but lived a long and happy life and enriched my childhood.

Never mind the expense, we would fight to the last to save

Suki, I said, and remembered with anguish those shivering balls of fur. Something must be done, I declared, and my vet said he would speak to the kennels' vet. Back home, I telephoned a town councillor who was, I knew, on the kennels' committee and asked her to visit the place and look into the matter. Suki's illness was disgusting and debilitating. The discharge from her nose was so copious I wore an old boiler suit when I handled her. If she tried to walk she fell over, so we carried her in and out of the garden to perform her natural duties. Angus, who liked his own way, was upset at being kept apart. His last year's distemper vaccination protected him from Suki's disease, but we were afraid he might try mating her. Then, as Suki fought for her life, her season ended abruptly and that worry was over.

Suki survived without any of the side-effects the vet had feared and by the time she was on the mend we had bonded closely. Henceforth she would not go out for walks with any other member of the family if I was around. She was a quick and instinctive learner. If I patted my leg and said "Heel" she obeyed at once, but, wanting to feel owned, she preferred to be on the lead in the street.

She adored Angus; every evening after their main meal the two of them went up to our bedroom to play, wrestling and growling, so ferociously that we called them the Dinosaurs.

In quieter moments Suki groomed Angus, licking the inside of his ears and combing his thick hair with her fine teeth. She copied his manners, never rushing to gobble up her dinner or stealing food at home, however hungry she might be. She learned not to take tidbits from strangers and to walk like him with an aristocratic air, so that when people asked what her breed was we invented one: "A tasselled Afghan hunting dog," we said.

But Angus had a naughty streak, too, which divided Suki's loyalties between him and us. She fetched him one day at our request when he had obstinately gone the wrong way down a track, proudly leading him back by a short piece of rope dangling from his collar. But he must have indicated his annoyance for she would never repeat this useful exercise. The crunch came when we left them alone in the house for three hours one evening and Angus decided to take his revenge with Suki's help. We returned home to find the hall carpet rolled up against the front door. When we eventually got inside the house the dogs slunk away guiltily, tails down, while we looked on the havoc they had wrought: torn tea towels, rugs rolled up; our daughter's slippers brought downstairs and chewed. Later Angus threw us a sideways glance which clearly said "serves you right," but Suki was so mortified by our anger that her confidence in him was dented and he was never able to enlist her help again.

Perhaps it was Suki's basic composure which made her so different from other dogs, a calmness which allowed her to sum up situations and listen carefully when she was addressed. The number of human words she understood quickly multiplied. And she had a remarkable capacity to make the most of every expedition, loving both the town, where she quickly acquired many canine friends, and the country, where Angus taught her how to handle cattle. Unlike him, she loved swimming and chasing rabbits and looking out of the car window as we drove around. Unlike him, too, she did not unpack shopping in the back of the car in the hope of finding ham, the only food Angus ever stole.

When Angus grew old Suki looked after him even more assiduously, acting as his eyes and ears, but she accepted his gradual muscle wastage, senility and eventual death with equanimity. Soon afterwards we moved to Chiswick, four miles from central London, where she immediately collected a circle of friends on the local Greens.

By now Suki was so civilised I could take her anywhere and she became my constant companion when I travelled across the country researching a book on prime ministers' consorts. She stayed with me in hotels. She visited stately homes and met Lord Home and his much loved Labrador at The Hirsel. She sat by my chair when I lunched in pubs. She accompanied me to Chiswick dress shops and lay contentedly outside changing cubicles while I tried on dresses. Like most dogs she was interested in clothes because they signalled what I was about to do. Dog-walking clothes were always welcomed, but high heels and evening dresses lowered her tail. The in-betweens were, like suitcases, a source for watchfulness and uncertainty, until I told her whether or not she was "coming."

One example of how Suki always got the best out of everything was her love for our children's pets, which she would watch for hours, and wash if she had the opportunity. She found guinea pigs so adorable that when she discovered that a neighbour down the road had a pen full of them, she would refuse to pass the gate until she had been allowed in to sit among them. When our son brought back a white-hooded Norwegian rat which he had saved from the ferrets at a nature centre where he worked as a volunteer, Suki could not have been happier. Ratty became a friend and perhaps as far as possible, a surrogate puppy.

Another human occupation Suki adored was house-hunting. Before we moved from the Midlands to London, she accompanied us round countless houses with excited interest. Whenever possible she liked to examine views from the windows. Bathrooms were also especially important to her—she would run back to take a quick recce if she thought we had missed one out. Sometimes we had to control her nosiness to avoid causing offence. Occasionally it was clear she hated a partic- ular house, perhaps sensing some past tragedy or distrusting the owners.

"Suki hated the vibes in that one," we would say afterwards.

The place we bought had a small, almost bare, paved gar- den with one border where Suki quickly made herself a small bower. We were afraid she might be depressed by the lack of space, but there was a bonus—a black Pekinese, Tato, who lived next door, a dog of impeccable pedigree and minute ap- petite. Tato's Greek owner fed him on a menu fit for a king and there were always leftovers, which in time, became Suki's. We met Tato on our morning walks, but I suspect it was the smell of Mediterranean cooking which tempted Suki to slip through the fence and make cautious overtures to his owner, which led to little dishes of leftovers being put before her. And so, al- though she had moved to London, Suki's life soon became full with weekends in the country and trips to Richmond Park with the canine friends she had made.

And then there was Christmas, that annual event which Suki looked forward to with increasing anticipation as soon as she saw presents being wrapped in fancy paper. The arrival and decoration of the tree increased her happy excitement. On the day she shared the children's Christmas stockings before running downstairs to look for her own bag of goodies.

Lunch with my sister, Josephine, meant more presents for Suki and a dinner party in the evening at our house provided her with guests to welcome, for Angus, who had perfected the art of canine host, had taught her how to greet visitors and, if they were staying, escort them to their rooms.

Josephine was a special friend because she looked after Suki when we went abroad and knew how to lighten her depression when we left. Then, encouraged, Suki would shake herself several times before settling down to enjoy her stay. Three days a week she went with Josephine to the Pen Club and became accustomed to office life. She sat in on committee meetings, elegantly draping herself across a chair, and grew used to different walks, for, above all, she was adaptable.

By now Suki had perfected her stares, those vital expressions dogs use to manipulate human beings. There was the astonished stare, eyes large, ears up, to express amazed disappointment when an expected morsel has not been offered; the reproachful stare, eyes mournful, ears down when a dog is about to be left at home; the hopeful stare (so hard to refuse) when Suki made it clear she expected your generosity. All these stares were guaranteed to make all but the most hard-hearted feel bad if they did not comply with the dog's wishes. And Suki was now following the usual progress of a well-treated domestic dog: four years servant, four years equal, four years tyrant; only she was the most charming tyrant, no barking, no bullying, just persuasive pleading and stares.

As Suki grew older her pleasures changed. She stopped chasing rabbits but adored visiting friends. If there was tea she gently indicated that she should have some in a saucer, and, this lapped-up carefully, she would nudge me until I asked whether she might go upstairs to explore. Then, admission granted, we would hear her hurrying from room to room, stopping to look out of windows; sometimes, halfway down, she would realise she had once again forgotten to examine the bathroom, and then she would go back and look in the bath. At some point, if the weather was fine, she asked to walk in the garden. Finally, after an hour, she would nudge me again, suggesting it was time we left.

Was Suki, I wondered, ever fantasising about another move? She liked our London house, but found it cold, which prompted reproachful stares and the pathetic sight of a small spaniel-like figure sitting very close to an unswitched-on electric fire. If she was, her wish came true, for now that our children were nearly grown-up, we decided to sell our country cottage and buy a larger London house. And to Suki's joy another search began.

We chose a house in the same area with a larger garden. It had very efficient central heating and was carpeted throughout, and Suki could see a resident squirrel from some of the windows. We left her with Josephine for a couple of days while the move took place, and when Josephine brought her back she knew exactly where we were. For, although she had visited the house only twice and Josephine had to park the car some distance away, Suki dragged her at the gallop to our new address. Had she heard us say this was the house we wanted? By now she certainly understood more of our conversation than we would once have believed possible.

Installed in the new house, Suki missed Tato, but loved the carpets and the heating, and never again asked that an electric fire be switched on. It was a good place in which to grow old, nearer to the Greens where she loved to meet her friends, and with a wide gentle staircase. And there was a bonus when our son rescued a white mouse wandering in the road. He made it an adventure playground in a large fish tank, and Suki, whom we always felt wanted a pet of her own, spent many hours watching it jumping from branch to branch and running in and out of toilet-roll tunnels. So the years passed and by now this dog who had come to us an ill, forsaken crossbreed of doubt-ful parentage, from horrible kennels, had won our hearts with a mixture of sensitive perception, lasting gratitude, an under-standing that touched on telepathy and an abiding wish to please. In some ways, I suspect, she knew us better than we knew ourselves.

There came a time when I wanted to describe her success on paper, which I did in the form of a letter written by an old dog, Suki, to a puppy on how to manipulate human beings and thus achieve complete canine contentment. It was published as a book and Suki posed for publicity photographs, sitting in a chair gazing thoughtfully at a typewriter, turning a typewritten page with her nose and visiting a post-box. The publishers gave a launch party for the book on one of the Greens. Forty-one dogs came, all her friends, but one—the local vet's liver-coloured labrador who could open a tin of dog meat with his teeth. It was too much. Suki, overwhelmed but still composed, moved away from everyone until her paw was needed to guide the knife that cut the celebratory cake.

She lived another two years, growing rather deaf and blind, but enjoying walks on a lead and still able to manage her life well in her own house. We never knew her birth date but when she died she must have been only a few weeks from her six-teenth birthday. She had watched our children grow up and to me her death seemed to herald the end of an era in our lives.

from BEST-LOVED DOG STORIES

The Heart Knows Best

"It is humanity's sympathy with
all creatures that first makes
us truly human."

ALBERT SCHWEITZER

*I*t's not surprising that hospitals and nursing homes are beginning to welcome visits from pets. Animals have a way of sensing people's needs, and they offer the best possible medicine: love. Perhaps you've received some from the animals you know. Perhaps a time of sadness was lifted when a dog pushed his head under your hand and you realized that someone cared. Or, when you were overcome with fear and worry, and happened to see a mother bird teaching her young ones how to find seeds in the grass, you found reason to hope. A kitten playing with your shoelaces can absolutely banish gloom.

Real Cowboys Don't Cry

LENTON McCLENDON

Growing up in a cattle and farming area, I had the opportunity on many occasions to help my father and uncles pull calves from cows who were having trouble giving birth. We would work feverishly for what seemed like a long time to save the lives of the cow and calf. When it was finally over, the cow would turn to see her baby. Pulling it close with her head, she would begin to clean it and allow it to nurse.

There was one time, however, when I was about 10 years old, when we gave our best effort, but the calf was born dead. As the cow turned to see her baby, the look in her eyes upon seeing that lifeless form was the most heart-wrenching thing I had ever seen. I remember thinking, *I'm going to cry!* so I ran around to the back of the pickup truck. To my surprise, I saw my father and Uncle Bryan coming from the other direction. They were wiping sweat out of their eyes, because "real cowboys don't cry."

Quickly we went to a nearby town that was having a cattle sale that day. After purchasing an orphaned newborn calf, we wiped the new calf with the gunnysack we'd used to wipe the dead calf, and went back to our pasture. Finding the cow wandering around in a daze, we unloaded the calf from the truck. Immediately the cow ran to it. Smelling the calf, she pulled it to her side and it began to nurse. I'm sure the cow knew deep down that this wasn't her true born, but she didn't care. She had love to give a baby and that baby needed a mother.

About 35 years later, my wife and I had the inexpressible joy of adopting our only child, a son. When they brought the most beautiful two-day-old baby boy I had ever seen into that room, I saw the look of love and satisfaction on my wife's face, and I remembered that day on the farm. I had to turn away quickly to wipe the sweat from my eyes, because "real cowboys don't cry."

Bunny Rab

ANNE WATKINS

"The dogs found 'em," my father-in-law explained as he placed the tiny, squeaking bundle in my hands. "Don't know where their mama went."

I stared in dismay at the tiny baby bunny squirming around in the palm of my hand. He was so new that his eyes were still sealed shut. My sisters-in-law gathered around us when they heard of the motherless bunnies, and each agreed to take one of the other four babies home with them. My bunny nudged helplessly at my finger and squealed. My heart melted. I had no idea how to take care of this tiny creature, but I was going to give it my best shot.

The first thing to do was feed the starving little rabbit. Not having any idea how to concoct a suitable formula, I mixed up a bit of evaporated milk with a little water and sugar. I warmed it, careful not to get it too hot, and put it in a doll's bottle. The bunny took to it as if it was the best food in the world! After he ate, he crawled up the front of my blouse and snuggled into my hair. In a few minutes he was sleeping, warm and soft, against my skin.

I was seven months pregnant and under doctor's orders to stay off my feet. Up until then I had been feeling useless and bored. The helpless baby rabbit placed in my care gave me something to think about besides myself. Sitting very still so as not to disturb the sleeping little one, I carefully stroked his velvety soft fur. He captured my heart with his trust and dependence. I decided to name my new friend Rab.

Amazingly, over the next few weeks, the orphan bunny began to grow and thrive. His eyes opened a short time after he came to be with me, and he was soon lapping his formula out of a jar lid, scorning the doll bottle. Out of all the babies found by the dogs that day, Rab was the only one to live. My father-in-law didn't seem to be the least surprised by Rab's survival. "I knew if anybody could do anything for him, you could," he said.

Before long, Rab was eating hamster pellets and treats. He was growing like a weed but was still so small! I usually put him in the bathroom when it was meal time for the rest of us and one night was surprised to see Rab sitting just outside the dining room. He was so tiny that he crawled right out under the bathroom door and came looking for me.

One of his favorite things to do was to climb up my blouse and nestle in my hair. He would often nuzzle my neck and make quiet little noises to himself before he fell asleep. These nap times were so precious to me. I'd sit very still and enjoy the feeling of his soft furry body against my skin. I knew it wouldn't be too long before he'd be too big for this and I wanted to enjoy it as long as I could.

Rab enjoyed stretching out in a patch of sun on the carpet, where he'd snooze until he got hungry and woke up. One day he hopped over to the front door and discovered some sand that had been tracked in onto the threshold. He immediately dropped to his side and began rolling back and forth in it. He was taking a dust bath! I couldn't help but laugh as I watched.

By the time my due date arrived, Rab was pretty big. He ate

hamster pellets all the time now, and had been weaned off the formula. He enjoyed gnawing on the hamster chew sticks I got him and was ready to start spending time outside. My husband built a nice roomy cage for Rab and set it up in the front yard. I was going to miss having him in the house but it had become too difficult for me to take care of him inside. We moved him into his new home and he immediately settled in, eating the soft green grass that poked up through the wire floor of the cage.

After a few days outside, Rab seemed content to sleep in the wooden house in the corner of the cage and to lap his water from a doggy bowl. I was pleased with how well he had taken to living outdoors. He was still as tame as ever and loved to hop over for a head scratch. The neighbor kids enjoyed visiting him.

One day when the little girl next door came to visit, she brought her big Irish setter with her. Seeing Rab, the dog began barking excitedly and charged right up to the cage. Without so much as a squeak, Rab dropped over onto his side. He never moved again.

Everyone told me that he must have died immediately from fright. My only consolation was that it happened so suddenly that he didn't have time to feel any pain. We buried him in the back yard and marked his grave with a pretty stone. I have never forgotten my brief time with that precious little soul who was so suddenly thrust into my care.

Rab, thank you for visiting with me!

Just the Same

KATHERINE L. HALL

I can remember going to pick out our first family dog when I was only six years old. That tiny ball of fur tucked in the straw of a barn laid the foundation for a canine love affair that I am sure will last my lifetime. Dogs were my constant childhood companions, co-explorers and confidants in the Colorado foothills I came to call home.

When I left home to begin my own life, I vowed to have my own dog as soon as I could. College, marriage and apartment living kept me from that goal for seven years, but I persisted (as my husband, Dwayne, can attest) and one week after we bought our first home, I got my wish. Sadie, the "dog of my dreams," was a year-old Chow/Shepherd mix that we adopted from a local shelter. She was worth the wait—smart, playful, protective and, above all, as grateful to have me as I was to have her.

Sadie opened my eyes to the plight of homeless pets and the amazing love and gratitude they have to offer. I was shocked to learn about the thousands of animals that are either abused, abandoned, or both, in this country each year. How could people be so heartless? How could they harm or neglect these magnificent creatures?

Two years later, Dwayne and I awoke to find "Inga" sitting

on our doorstep. She was a three-month-old Husky/Chow mix pup with some very obvious problems: patchy, sparse hair, runny eyes and a belly full of worms. Inga was a real "ugly pupling!" The kids next door told me that she had been roaming our neighborhood for days. After several trips to the veterinarian, Inga's health and appearance improved dramatically. She sprouted hair like a Chia pet, and her cheerful demeanor through it all was captivating. It wasn't long before Inga wiggled her way right into our family and our hearts.

Three years ago, we all moved to Rifle, a small community on the western slope of Colorado. We love being closer to the mountains. There are more places to ride our motorcycles and, of course, to take Sadie and Inga, too!

I also had the opportunity to become involved in a local effort to improve the city dog pound. It was starting to deteriorate, and the Department of Agriculture had given it a three-month deadline to make the necessary repairs or be closed down. Here was my chance to get involved in something I really cared about and to work with others who felt the same. Our little group, the Friends of the Rifle Animal Shelter, held fundraisers, solicited donations, labor and materials, and all rolled up our shirt-sleeves to help. I was even able to convince my motorcycle-loving husband to spare a few weekends and do a little plumbing work up there. We were able to make the required repairs and even add improvements to make our shelter a more comfortable place for the animals and human visitors, too.

I became an adoption volunteer. Finding loving homes for abandoned animals gave me a wonderful feeling that I was closer to the Lord.

Last fall, the number of dogs at the shelter hit an all-time high. Adoptions had dropped off, and many of the dogs had been there for several weeks. It was depressing, and I kept having this nagging feeling that I should be doing more. Maybe, we could adopt a third dog? It would make things a little tight, but I became convinced it was what I needed to do. I prayed, and pestered poor Dwayne. Sadie and Inga weren't "spring chickens" anymore and I didn't want them to feel slighted or overwhelmed. It would take just the right dog. Slowly, I began to take note of a red adolescent Husky at the shelter. His coat was a mess but he was very affectionate and his bright blue eyes captivated me. I was impressed with his ability to get along with all the other dogs and he behaved well on a leash. He had been there for over three weeks, yet as sweet as he was, no one had shown any interest in him. After bragging about him to another volunteer, it dawned on me that he was the dog I had been looking for.

Dwayne and I decided to bring "Luke" home the next night. He instantly adored Sadie and Inga! They were a bit taken aback by his youthful exuberance but it was easy to see that they really liked him and his puppy antics. He was eager to please and curious about everything. The next day he got a much-needed bath and we all spent a lot of time playing and just getting to know one another.

Later that evening, Dwayne was washing dishes while I wrote a letter. Luke was in the kitchen with Dwayne. I glanced in their direction and saw Luke's head fly back, his mouth open wide, and then he rolled onto his back. His limbs began to flail wildly. Luke was having a seizure! He convulsed for about two minutes before becoming limp. He was disoriented, frightened and didn't recognize his surroundings or us. He spent the next 45 minutes pacing about, running into things and panting heavily. When he finally stopped, he fell asleep.

We were stunned! It was now painfully clear why Luke had been abandoned. A cloud hung over the rest of the evening, and very little was said before going to bed. Around two a.m., Luke experienced another seizure, followed by a third at six a.m. I called Karen, the shelter's veterinarian, and she came right over. No one had ever seen his seizures before, and Karen could tell I was shaken. She made arrangements for Luke to go to a local clinic that morning.

As I drove Luke there, my mind was a blur. I was trying to do a good thing—Why was this happening? The veterinarian examined Luke and said that his seizures could have numerous causes. It would take extensive testing to narrow them down. He also informed me that, left untreated, his seizures could cause permanent brain damage or death. Then he went on to say that earlier in the year a couple had brought in a red Husky puppy. It had also been experiencing seizures. When they were given his prognosis, the couple decided to return him to the breeder. The vet was convinced that Luke was the same dog.

I decided to leave Luke at the clinic overnight for observation, some preliminary testing and, honestly, to give myself some time to think. This was not what I had prayed for. As Dr. Smith led Luke to a kennel in the back, he was no longer that playful pup who had entertained and charmed all of us just hours before. Luke's head hung down, his eyes were dull and he barely shuffled along. Not once did he look back at me. As the doors swung shut, I suddenly realized that I was "just the same." I was the same as all the other people Luke had given his heart to and then, when his condition became apparent, had left him. I was the same as those who had left both Sadie and Inga years ago. I was letting my fear and disappointment blind me to Luke's needs. I was no better than others who had found it easier to walk away than to try to help this poor creature. I cried all the way home. I prayed aloud, asking God to help Luke and to help me find the strength to see things through.

That evening Dwayne and I talked about the commitment it would take to meet Luke's needs, and I was pleased to find that he felt, as I did, that we should do all we could.

The next two months were difficult. There were many more trips to the veterinarian, more medical tests, new treatments and more seizures. The Friends of the Rifle Animal Shelter group helped with expenses, and Luke was even on our prayer chain at church. Eventually we would find ourselves taking Luke to the veterinary program at Colorado State University. There Luke was diagnosed with epilepsy and placed on daily medication. He will always have to take it but, with proper monitoring, he should lead a normal life.

That was six months ago and Luke hasn't had another seizure. In all likelihood, he will, but they should not be harmful and we are now more prepared to handle them. Luke's personality has blossomed. He has become the "family clown," entertaining us with his toys, wrestling with Sadie and Inga and taking daily dips in his wading pool. He is grateful and so am I.

I have learned an important lesson in humility and understanding. It is now my turn to help others in similar situations find the strength and hope God gives us to handle difficult situations, even when it comes to our pets!

God has granted us dominion over the animals. They are counting on us to use it with commitment and compassion.

A Special Greeting

EDWARD GRINNAN

My little dog Sally Brown teaches me many things, and as usual I learn in spite of myself. The other day on my lunch hour I was impatiently walking her around the block (dragging might be a better word). I didn't have much time, and I let her know it. But cocker spaniels have relentless noses.

Around the corner came a man—I'm tempted to say old man, but there was really no telling—dressed in a soiled and ragged overcoat, grubby strands of dark hair half-tucked up under a frayed watch cap, his eyes sagging and sad. I, a seasoned New Yorker, glanced away.

But Sally made a kind of scurrying beeline to him, her stubby remnant of a tail vibrating in excitement. It was an utter mystery to me why she picked out this sorry soul to greet with the joy of a long-lost friend. My hand tightened on the leash. I wanted to pull her back, but self-consciousness got the better of me and I slackened my grip.

Sally sat demurely, obligingly allowing herself to be adored and stroked by the grimy hands. She gazed up at her admirer appreciatively. His features softened, a spark ignited in his eyes, and he smiled. "You *beeeaauutiful* girl, you!" he exclaimed quietly. "Thanks for saying hello."

He never looked at me. Quickly, he straightened up and was off. I stood and watched the man disappear down the street, wondering how he would have responded if it had been I who had stopped to say hello.

Gus, the Big White Dog

BRENDA RANDOLPH

Teaching a unit on Alaska and the Iditarod race to a building filled with K–2nd graders in rural Missouri in springtime may sound a little far-fetched to some, but via the internet plus other hands-on materials and movies, this was an annual event that the students in our school loved.

The children chose a musher to root for, learned all about lead dogs, swing dogs and living in the Arctic. One particular little boy who was normally very introverted came alive in this unit and was in awe of everything we had learned right down to watching the Disney movie "Iron Will."

The movie portrayed a teenage boy racing for the prize money to save the family farm. He had his deceased father's large white Husky, Gus, leading his team. Evan seemed attracted like a magnet to this unit and especially the movie. Since he was such a quiet child, it happened to be one of the few times he shared his school activities with his parents. Each day he kept them updated as to what we were doing in class and how his musher was doing. His parents were thrilled to see him taking so much interest.

This year, as always, not only was I busy at school, but my

husband had been transferred to another part of the state. I had stayed behind to finish the school year and then would make a 3-hour commute to spend the weekends with my husband and sons.

One Sunday evening, en route from Southeast Missouri back to the Ozarks and school on Monday, I came up on a ramp and saw a large white Husky lying in the middle of my lane. As I swerved, I realized the animal was injured. He didn't even try to get up. He just raised his head so pitifully and seemed to stare me in the face, as if to say, "Do something!" Normally I wouldn't stop for an injured or stray animal for fear of what the animal might do, but strangely enough, I found myself pulling off to the side. I watched as other cars swerved to avoid him. Then I decided to use my cell phone and call 911 for someone to come and rescue him.

As I waited for help, I decided to get out and try to coax the dog off to the side of the road. All the time, I wondered, *What am I doing?* I thought my humanitarian instincts might have been running wild after watching that movie "Iron Will" with my students. It never even occurred to me that the dog might bite. He just looked so pitiful with those big dark round eyes and all that white fur.

By then a young city policeman showed up, complete with plastic gloves, etc., and asked me some questions. "Has he been aggressive? Can he crawl?"

"No," I said, "but we have to get him off the road or, as big as he is, he could cause an accident."

At that moment, a trucker pulled up behind my van and got out. He started flagging traffic for us as we discussed what we should do. The policeman begged me to take the dog. He explained that if he took him to the pound, they would put him down, for sure. Well, I certainly didn't want him put down because by that time I felt like the dog's guardian angel or something.

I tried to explain that I was not able to keep him because my family and home were strung out across the state. I was headed back to my parents home where I was staying during the week. It was another hour away and I had no idea whether the dog would even make it. Or what he might do if he woke up in the van.

When the policeman learned where I was headed, he said he was from that same little town of 700 people. He just knew I could find someone there who would take the dog in and give him plenty of room to run.

I finally succumbed to the policeman's pleas. We lifted the dog into the back of my van and I set out once again. This time I called the farm for someone to meet me at the barn in about an hour.

My dad and brother were waiting for me, both of them shaking their heads at me. Then they took a look at the white Husky. "His back is probably broken," my dad said. "If he's still alive by morning and not up on his feet, we'll dispose of him for you. He's definitely not a cow dog, so we won't keep him. Should he get better, you'll have to find a home for him."

Fair enough, I thought, not having a clue what I'd do with the dog if he did survive.

We placed him in a pen. I gave him a bowl of water, sat with him for awhile and turned in for the night.

Morning came. I rushed to the kitchen window to peer out. The dog wasn't up. Disappointed, I sat down at the breakfast table with my parents. Dad had already been up and had seen that the dog hadn't moved all night. I soon realized that Dad was beginning to falter on the deal about putting him down. He had come up with Plan B! He said, "How about I'll drop him off on the vet's doorstep and leave a note? It will say, 'A nice lady picked me up off the highway. If you can't fix me, just put me out of my misery. If you can, please fix me and get me adopted.'"

I immediately grinned and quickly scratched the note on a small piece of paper for him. We went out the door together and he loaded the dog as I left for school.

When I got to school that morning, I shared my story with my kindergarteners, who nick-named the dog "Gus" from the Disney movie they had just seen.

Evan, the quiet little red-headed boy, cornered me later and whispered, "Mrs. Randolph, if Gus gets better, can I have him? I have a farm with lots of room for him." I was so touched, I nearly cried. "Well, Evan, you'll have to get permission from your parents, but I would be glad for you to have Gus."

That afternoon, the class wanted to check on Gus, so we all trooped down to the office to use the speaker phone. This way everyone could hear the conversation between the veterinarian and me. I dialed the vet to inquire about the big white Husky, and in a very cold professional manner, he told me he would not treat Gus until I gave my name and address so he would know where to send the bill. One of my little boys who has not discovered r's in the English language yet, blurted out, "Heuah name is Mrs. Wandolph! and we live at Koshkonong!"

"OK!" I told the vet. "Fix Gus, and I'll pay!" I couldn't say no and break the hearts of my whole class! They would never understand.

After examining Gus, the veterinarian called back. He said, "Fortunately, Gus's back was not broken. However, his shoulder was out of place and would need surgery to put it back in. The cuts and scrapes on his legs were minor."

As the days wore on, the bills kept mounting. But it was amazing how so many students, teachers, and friends soon learned about Gus. Suddenly God's love came pouring in through the form of monetary donations to help with Gus's surgery, medical care and hospital stay.

Evan and his mother began visiting the vet's office daily, and the bond between boy and dog began to grow. At the end of Gus's hospital stay, he was adopted by Evan and his family.

Today, Gus has a little red-headed freckled boy, a family, and a large farm with lots of animals to play with. He has made a full recovery. Gus returns his love and appreciation to his newfound family by catching turtles for them. He places them upside down on the family's front porch as his way of saying, "Thank you for my new life."

God loves the animals as well as the children, so sometimes it takes a community of faith to bring one of his plans together. I believe this story to be one of those special plans created by the Master himself.

Waiting for Friendship

PHYLLIS HOBE

Why won't he look at me?

For a month I had been working as a volunteer at a center for mentally challenged children, and Jim—one of the children assigned to me—wasn't responding at all. Each time I visited, he simply stared at the television.

I tried everything. I showed him brightly colored balls, urged him to jump rope, offered him a bicycle to ride—but he only turned away. I worried incessantly about him—he was so alone, so friendless.

Then one day I brought my dog Trooper to work with me. Jim's eyes brightened the moment he saw the dog. Trooper sniffed all around Jim's room, the way dogs will, and once acquainted with his surroundings, he curled up at Jim's feet in front of the television set.

I left them together and went on to do other things.

When I returned an hour later, Trooper was peacefully curled up in Jim's lap, lying there quietly as Jim gently patted his head and whispered into his ear. They were friends!

Now why haven't I been able to draw some of that love from Jim? I asked myself. Because I had tried to force my friendship on him rather than simply let him be, as Trooper did, until he reached for me.

The Lost Dog

GENE HILL

---

*E*very time I stopped, the moonlight seemed to carry the slight tinkle of the dog bell I was listening for so intently. I stood there, heron-like, one foot in the air, afraid to put it down for fear that the slightest noise might mute the one sound I was waiting for. But the evening was a mocking one—I felt I might well have been searching for a leprechaun or stalking the pot of gold at the end of a rainbow.

I had last seen Pat at about 10 A.M. when she had found and pointed a woodcock. When I shot, she broke, as usual, since I wasn't too meticulous on that nicety, and up in front of us flushed a prime whitetail buck. Before this Pat had been at worst a five-minute deer chaser, just a little run to satisfy her instincts. I hadn't been overly concerned, but this time as they flashed through the woods I had the feeling that five minutes wouldn't get the job done. Twelve hours later, as worried as I was angry, proved my hunch.

As English Setters go, Pat wasn't your "once-in-a-lifetime dog." She was stubborn, willful, and vain. But I had trained her to the point where, when all went well, I could get a decent day's shooting over her. But when all didn't go well it could be a disaster. Many days I simply gave up and led her back to the kennel in the station wagon deciding to do the best I could by myself. I guess I kept her out for a variety of self-indulgent reasons: my refusal to admit I hadn't done as good a job of training as I should have; my tendency to spoil her and overlook the little hardheaded acts that usually led to bigger transgressions; and my plain softheartedness in refusing to come down harder and more often—a practice which might or might not have made a difference.

But by 10 P.M. all I could think of was a hurt dog lying in a roadside ditch waiting for me to find her, or a dog in the bottom of an abandoned well listening to my call and whistle and her answering bark tumbling back down on her in hollow, miserable mockery. I envisioned her collar hung on a wire fence, her foot in a forgotten fox trap. Anger and self-pity slowly gave way to fear and frustration so strong it nearly made me sick to my stomach. It was I who was the guilty one now and she the one needing desperately to have me with her.

I sat there listening to the night sounds . . . jet planes I'd rather have had been north winds. I'd rather the horns and screeching tires to have been the night calling of geese and herons. The sense of loss grew. Nothing comforted me. Everything seemed wrong. I felt like a small and simple man looking and listening for a lost dog while an impersonal, mechanical world went right on by without stopping to help or pausing to care.

The next day I told a friend I was upset about losing my dog, but he paid no attention to my grief; dogs are not worldly goods. That night I returned to where I had left my hunting coat with the slight belief that Pat would be there waiting for me. But the coat was an empty mockery of hope. I whistled and listened through yet another night, not knowing what else to do. Anxiety and fear were shoved aside by a feeling of futility and helplessness. The airplanes and traffic sounds made me feel more alone than ever before. I was on some strange sort of island.

I called the police but they showed little interest in only a lost dog. A check of neighboring houses and farms led to nothing. They promised to call if they saw a white English Setter but somehow I didn't feel encouraged. To them I was just an annoying stranger with a petty problem. I was a suspicious character to several, disbelieved by others, and, in my mind, ignored by all.

By now the night vigil had taken on another emotional aspect for I was searching for an unknown thing. Pat had become a symbol as real as any physical being. I needed to find her not only because I was committed to ending the mystery, but because I wanted to take her to these uncaring people and say, in effect, "Here is the dog I asked you about. See how much we enjoy each other; do you understand now how much it meant for me to have your help and understanding?" I wanted them to learn something about strangers and lost dogs and kindness, and caring enough to listen to the hurt of others with sympathy.

There was little sense in wandering around since Pat, no doubt, was doing the same thing, so I decided instead to find a spot to use as a post. I chose a long, slanting, fallen oak whose branches had caught in another tree. I climbed up, rested my back against a limb, and watched the evening mist beneath me like a silken sea. Here, suspended in space and time, my imagination was free to create a scene of a dog running a deer for a day, then, just as she is about to give up and come home another deer jumps in front of her, and then another. Unable to stop herself, Pat is lead into a land she can never leave. I imagined a dog barking and another answering, then a third calling. My imagination flowed freely once again. One dog started barking and then dogs all across the country answered one another in an endless chain of howls in recognition of all that dogs have suffered at the hands of man in the cold light of the moon. I listened for a dog calling my name.

I placed a small ad in the local paper: LOST DOG, my name and telephone number, a description of Pat and the promise of a reward, but I had no faith in it. Almost a week had passed and I was running out of things to do; yet I felt I had to do something. The fading moon was just a twist of yellow like a discarded rind of lemon, making the night seem ominous. I brought a star book, laid back on my oak bed, and tried to memorize the Pleiades, Orion, and Betelgeuse. I thought of the ancient desert shepherds and their nighttime philosophies on the stars. I thought of their naked minds relating the unrelatable, glibly marrying suspicion, myth, and astrology, and trying to find a meaningful place for themselves while being surrounded by nothing except the incredible extension of their intellect. And I was bewildered when I thought how much of it had really worked out after all. But, in the long run, philosophy is a comfort only to philosophers and I am not really one of those incredible abstract thinkers—just a small, cold man lost in the woods being hunted, I hoped, by a hungry, homesick bird dog.

I tried the old hunters trick of imagining what I would do if I was a lost dog. Where would I go? What would be the limits of my endurance? But this was idle foolishness. Pat could literally be anywhere—around the next turn or in another world. The night vigil had lost its feeling of function and I took to driving around more and sitting less. A pointless use of time perhaps, but maybe, just maybe, I would find Pat.

I gave up when over a week had passed. I took the kennel out of the station wagon and avoided going near the dog run by the barn. My family had long since stopped talking about hunting in an effort to be kind to me, but it didn't matter. My own feelings were mixed: a sense of loss, a deep guilt, and worst of all, a nagging uncertainty. I didn't really believe Pat was gone. I couldn't conceive or cope with the idea of forever. I still drove around the area where she had run away, but more like a person trying to wake up from a bad dream than from any real hope of seeing her sitting by the side of the road listening for the familiar sound of my car. People would recognize my car and wave, and a couple of kids knew me as the "lost dog man."

My mind searched for a simple solution. I imagined Pat had been hit by a passing car, then crawled into the woods and gone to sleep, undetected by the driver. It was neat, logical, likely—and unsatisfactory. Other possibilities came to mind but none were any better.

After two weeks the painful sense of loss faded, leaving a numb feeling of emptiness. I still caught myself listening for her bark when I pulled in the driveway, but the empty spots where she used to lie seemed ordinary again and I didn't think about feeding time anymore. I felt better when I reminded myself that she was just an ordinary working field dog, nothing to brag about, spoiled, mischievous—and yet it hurt to remember that Pat was my dog in every sense of the word. She followed me everywhere, slept by my chair when I let her in the house and loved riding in the front seat of the car. The simple truth was that Pat had gotten to me in her own way, more than I had been readily willing to admit before. I felt almost ashamed to be so sentimental. It was difficult to imagine a man my age cry-ing alone in his car for the sight of a small white dog. But it happened, and happened more than once.

This was all some time ago and I've never seen or heard of Pat again. I'm past grief now. Her image in my memory remains like a poorly focused snapshot of a white dog off in an alder thicket—indistinct and distant like a ghost or a drifting wraith of mist.

They say that time heals all wounds, but that's not wholly true. Sometimes we can work around the reality and believe in a hereafter when we have to—imagining a lost dog living with someone else far away—a kind and gentle master who has discovered that she loves to ride in the front seat of the car with the window open, hates peanut butter sandwiches, and will, for no apparent reason, cock her head and stand stock still for the longest time as if she were listening for a faint whistling carried on the evening wind and the calling of a name she still remembers.

from TEARS & LAUGHTER

Friends

STEPHANIE LALAND

*B*uffy and Tawnie were both Labrador-shepherd mix dogs who spent most of their time in the backyard. In the evening, they were invited indoors to share the life of the Gundran family. At night the two dogs would stay in the garage. As the two dogs lived into their thirteenth year, Tawnie suffered from back pain and Buffy gradually lost her sight.

Toward the end of Buffy's life, she began to suffer small strokes, yet each time she recovered enough to live on with some enjoyment. On the last night of her life, Buffy apparently wandered out of the garage and sat by the gate of the dog-run in the pouring rain. There she suffered a massive stroke.

The next morning it was still raining. The Gundrans went into the garage to say good morning to the dogs, but both were missing. When they finally searched outside, they found both dogs lying side by side in the downpour.

The Gundrans noted that the garage door had been open so that Tawnie could have taken shelter at any time during the night. But because Buffy's stroke had left her incapacitated, her dear friend Tawnie, though herself suffering from severe arthritis, chose to spend the entire night outdoors lying next to Buffy, trying to shield her from the rain and keep her warm. Both dogs were cold and soaked.

The Gundrans gently helped Buffy inside; Tawnie followed. Tawnie had suffered greatly through the long cold night but she had refused to leave the side of her lifelong buddy. "We think Tawnie knew that it was time for her friend to prepare to leave this earth, and so spent the last, long night by her side. I have a lump in my throat just writing this, but I feel I would like to share this with others," writes Ms. Gundran.

Tawnie had to consider what was most important on the last night of her friend's life. She decided it was not her own physical comfort. Even though she herself was plagued with crippling arthritis, she would not permit her friend to die alone. Throughout the long, cold, rainy night, the comfort and warmth of the garage lay just a few feet away, but Buffy could not even drag herself to it.

Tawnie proved that when someone needs you, that is all that matters.

from ANIMAL ANGELS

A Parrot Taught Me Her Song

RONALD L. HARMON

$\mathcal{S}$hortly after my mother passed away, my father was diagnosed with congestive heart failure. For ten years I helped my father, and every waking moment became filled with caregiving on top of a full-time job. It was difficult for me to give so much, but love for my father motivated me to do everything I could.

After Dad died I felt alone, as if my days couldn't get any darker. Yet, I soon realized a freedom I'd never experienced during all the years of helping my father. But this was tempered by the fact that because I'd spent so much time caring for someone, my life now seemed to take on a chilling sort of emptiness.

Friends suggested that I get a pet. I thought about the idea but didn't have a clue what kind of animal best suited me. A friend from Germany visited my home after staying with a family in Canada. He kept telling me about the clever little bird his Canadian hosts had. The idea of having a bird in the house began to sound wonderful. My friend assured me that birds are clean and easy to care for. He tried hard to convince me that I should consider getting a bird companion. But a married couple I knew had a parrot. While visiting them, their parrot's loud screams made me nervous. I knew that this sort of pet wouldn't work for me. I thought about the pros and cons of dogs, cats, even guinea pigs, but I decided a bird just didn't seem to be in my future.

One afternoon I went to a local shopping center and ambled into the pet store. Perched in the open near the front door sat an exquisite soft gray bird with a red tail. A couple of customers commented about how tame the little feathered creature seemed when the parrot allowed them to stroke her head. Suddenly, I found myself thinking, *I want this bird.* Immediately, though, I squelched the idea of buying a pet and left the store.

The image of the little gray bird stayed with me as my car seemed to float down the highway away from the store. Even names for the new pet drifted through my mind. After some thought, I settled on calling the bird Buddy. I'd driven about a mile or two along the highway when I decided to go back and buy Buddy no matter what the cost. That day began a relationship like none I'd ever thought could be possible with an animal.

As if in answer to my pre-Buddy loneliness, the bird liked to whistle for me when I left the room, never wanting me to be out of her sight for too long. If I didn't answer Buddy's whistle soon enough, she'd come looking for me. When friends dropped in, Buddy would climb down the ladder from the top of her cage to see who had stopped by. The minute my guests saw the little parrot she became the center of attention. My friends and I would sit on the floor and play with Buddy as she'd happily hop from one person to another lifting her foot to be picked up or performing some other trick to get our attention.

One of my favorite experiences with Buddy was how she responded to having me read stories to her while she was still too young to talk. Some nights I read stories substituting Buddy's name for one of the characters. She seemed thrilled and listened with childlike interest. Winter nights often felt cold and dark when I got off work, but because of Buddy, my little house loomed cozy and warm. The thought of this happy little bird being there filled my heart with gratitude. In the evenings I'd sit in the television room with Buddy perched nearby on a wooden hall tree. Together we'd watch television or listen to music in comfortable companionship.

When Christmas inched closer, with my family gone, I thought it could be a really difficult and sad occasion. One comfort was that Buddy and I would be celebrating the young parrot's first Christmas together. As the cold winter mornings edged their way toward Christmas, my little friend would sit on the top of her cage and sing as if thanking God for being alive. It surprised me when some of the Christmas carols became Buddy's favorites and she'd sing along to them. Buddy in her own way added something special only she could bring to the spirit of Christmas, and I loved her for it.

Buddy was four months old when we began sharing our lives together. When I first saw the lovely African grey at the pet store, I didn't know it, but Buddy was destined to fill a void in my existence. Because of my relationship with Buddy, I no longer suffered loneliness but experienced a true expression of God's love. Buddy's companionship gives me the lasting kind of gifts that make every day Christmas.

from ANGEL ANIMALS

A GENEROUS SPIRIT

"Love lifts us up where we belong."

JOE COCKER

Every now and then my animals have had to accept a newcomer. One reason is that my dog Suzy has a knack for finding lost and unwanted animals, and the only thing for me to do is bring them home.

The other animals aren't always welcoming to the newcomer. A certain amount of hissing and growling goes on—but only for a little while. Pretty soon Sean, my senior cat, gets down on the floor with the newcomer and begins swinging his tail. It makes a marvelous toy and before long the newcomer is playing with it and feeling right at home. Sean leads the way, but soon the others let down their guard and begin to teach the newcomer what family life is all about.

Griz

KRISTIN VON KREISLER

Griz, a hulking 650-pound grizzly bear, rooted around in his lunch at Wildlife Images, an animal rehabilitation center near Grants Pass, Oregon. In Griz's five-gallon feed bucket were apples, oranges, vegetables, kibble, chicken, and road-kill venison—a feast he was gobbling up with such pleasure that he did not notice a six-week-old, orange tabby kitten clamber under the fence into his pen.

The kitten, which weighed just over half a pound, had recently been dumped at the shelter and was forlorn and hungry. He cautiously stepped closer to Griz, sat down beside him, and meowed to ask for food.

As Griz looked up from his lunch and contemplated the tiny creature, Dave Siddons, the shelter's founder, watched in alarm. "Oh, God!" he thought. "Griz is going to eat that kitten!"

But Siddons would never be able to reach the kitten in time. At any moment, Griz would undoubtedly swat him and kill him for an extra bite of lunch. Siddons wished that bears were not omnivores.

Although Griz was an extremely sweet-natured animal, he could be just as violent as any bear when hunting for food. A train had slammed into him and damaged his brain when, as a cub, he'd foraged for spilled grain on a Montana railroad track.

A Native American tribe had crated him up and sent him, unconscious, to Siddons, who, along with his staff, had nursed and hand-fed Griz for weeks. After that coddling, the bear was too tame and gentle to survive in the wild.

Nevertheless, the bear was not so gentle that he would stop himself from killing the kitten. With gritted teeth, Siddons braced himself for a tragedy.

Griz looked down at the tabby and did nothing. Then he picked a chicken wing out of his pile of food, pulled off a little meat, and set it on the ground beside his paw for the kitten. The tiny creature pounced on the food and devoured it. Griz fed him a few more scraps.

Later that day, the kitten curled up on the bear's chest, in the crook of his arm, and napped with him. From then on, even after the kitten grew up and had acquired the name "Cat," Griz shared his food with him. They played together like the best of friends. Cat would conceal himself behind the pine trees in the bear's one-acre pen, then leap out and swat Griz's nose. The bear often carried Cat around in his mouth or let Cat ride on his back. Sometimes Griz licked Cat until he was clean, and at night they even slept together.

An unlikely friendship? Indeed. But proof that compassion may be the first step for animals—and humans—to live in harmony.

from THE COMPASSION OF ANIMALS

Sam and Sadie

SHARON SURBER

On a sunny day in Southern California, a little mutt named Sadie roamed the city streets. She had been on the streets for a couple of days and had but a few thoughts in mind—food, water, a warm bed, and lots of love. Well, I'll let her tell the rest of the story, since she's the one who really knows it best:

Here comes a pretty lady in a neat looking truck. Maybe she'll give me a ride to her house where I'll get lots of food and love. The lady picked me up and put me in her truck. Sitting next to me was the funniest looking dog I'd ever seen. She claimed to be a lhasa and poodle mix, but she had the longest body and the shortest legs. She said her name was Sam. I could tell she seemed a little nervous, and perhaps sensed trouble.

When the truck pulled up at our new home, I heard many of my own kind talking. Some sounded sorrowful and some very scared. What is this place where the truck has taken us? The sign on the front of the building read "Animal Shelter." The truck lady took me and Sam inside, and put us in kennels side by side. They gave us some food and water. I curled up next to the wire fence and Sam curled up next to me. We kept each other warm and secure.

As days passed, a few of our friends were taken out the

back door for walks, but never seemed to return. We wondered where they had gone! People came in the front door,
sometimes walking briskly up and down the aisles. They
seemed to be looking for something specific, I'm not sure
what. On this particular day, a nice looking couple came by my
cage and stopped for awhile. The man shook his head and
walked on, but the woman stayed a while looking at me. Oh, I
almost forgot, my name is Sadie. I tried to look cute, but I really
didn't know what I was supposed to do. They walked off, the
woman talking, but the man was still shaking his head. I
watched as they drove away.

I tried to get Sam to play with me, but she didn't seem very
interested. Most of the time she didn't even want to eat her dinner. Once in a while, the lady who picked us up in the truck
would open a kennel door and take my friends out for people
to see. They would be petted, and sometimes picked up and
held. I wanted someone to pick me up. The people and my
friends would walk out together and get in a car and drive
away. I thought they were so lucky!

A couple of days later, the woman and the man who visited
before came back, and they had the lady who drove the truck
with them. Maybe they were coming to see Sam and me. They
walked my way, and the next thing I knew, the truck lady was
opening my cage door. My heart was pounding wildly. They
patted me on the head, picked me up and I gave the woman a
lick. She smelled so good. The man was talking, but he didn't
seem to know what he wanted. They put me back in the cage
and walked down the aisles looking at my other friends. Then
they came back. The truck lady took me out of the cage and
put a rope around my neck.

As we walked away I noticed the truck lady didn't open

Sam's cage. *Wait! What about my friend Sam! You can't leave her here.* I tried not to walk, but they were dragging me. I kept looking back at Sam. She was my friend, I couldn't leave her here. The nice woman stopped and talked to the man. He shook his head no and kept pulling me along. They took me down the ramp and into an office where they filled out paperwork and paid for me. As we were getting ready to get into the car, I kept pulling at my new leash, pulling towards the kennels where Sam was barking and running up and down the cage wildly.

The truck lady kept looking at her watch and seemed impatient, as it was almost closing time. The man and woman talked to each other some more. Then, all three of us went back inside where Sam was jumping up and down at the kennel door. I couldn't believe it! The man motioned for the truck lady to open Sam's cage door. As the door opened, Sam jumped into the man's arms and gave him a big kiss. The man nodded yes and smiled at the woman. They took Sam and me back into the office and repeated the same procedure.

Sam and I and the nice couple all got into the car and went to our new home. That night as we were cuddling up in our warm beds to go to sleep, we overheard the man and woman talking. They were talking about how the truck lady told them they were planning to take me and Sam on one of those walks out the back door. The same ones we saw our friends go on that never returned. Our walk was scheduled for the following morning.

from UNFORGETTABLE MUTTS

Another Daisy

GENE HILL

$\mathcal{I}$t was close to Christmas, and that's why I think I had the whole wrong attitude. Bird hunting was far from my mind; our season was over for all practical purposes, and I had a lot of other things I was involved with. So when he drove down my lane in his pickup I was bothered by the intrusion and impatient for him to go.

He was anxious to chat about bird shooting and dogs and settled in oblivious or uncaring about my mood. He talked about his past season and, as usual, bragged heavily about his current crop of bird dogs. He was a Southern itinerant who did some mysterious thing for a living between bird seasons, but whatever it was he did, it seemed profitable enough because he always had a fairly new high-grade Browning 20-bore to show me and he affected exotic leather cowboy boots that were handmade and worth more than I would venture to guess.

I had seen several of his dogs in the field—he'd put them down on my farm before to show me how well they worked— and every one I'd seen was as close to perfection as I could imagine a dog to be. He would virtually never raise his voice above a whisper—just a tiny, almost imperceptible whistle every now and then, and the results were immediate and precise. Once he'd brought a dog he was trying to sell and put it down in an 8- or 10-acre section and the dog pointed and held at least six pheasants in about 15 minutes. If he went an inch out of his way from bird to bird, I surely didn't notice it. So when he talked about Honey, or Belle, or Duke I didn't question their prowess a bit.

As usual, he had a homemade kennel in the back of the truck and I knew by the way the conversation was going that he was again trying to sell me a dog. All the while he was describing how absolutely perfect the dog was, I was making up reasons in my mind to say *no*. He said that the dog with him was as good as he'd ever owned—and better than most he'd seen—but he needed money and since he preferred to hunt on horseback, the dog was a little too slow to suit his taste. He thought she'd be perfect for my walking-around gunning.

By now I'd calmed down, knowing that I was stuck with him for a few hours anyway, and he'd gotten my curiosity up to where I agreed to put the dog down in the section beyond the corn and watch her work. I knew there'd be a pheasant there late in the afternoon and I also knew that she'd never worked a pheasant before, so I was more than anxious to see what would happen.

I have, in more than twenty years of fooling around with all sorts of field dogs, seen it all. There have been the picture book paragons who were worthless and the snipe-nosed, indifferent looking dogs who had performed prodigies. But a given breed does have a few characteristics that we look for: a way of standing, a certain air of competence, an elan, a spark in the eyes. We like a dog that looks as if he can do what he was meant to do; as the architects put it, we expect form to follow function. The door of the wood-and-pig-wire kennel opened and nothing happened. No nose poked out. No eager barking. No sound. Nothing.

The owner acted not at all surprised, and chatted on until he'd finished whatever he was talking about. He turned and looked at the kennel and gave an almost inaudible whistle—a tiny expulsion of air that lay somewhere between a sound and imagining one. Then, slowly and tentatively, blinking her eyes at the light as if she had been in total darkness for months, emerged what you accepted as a pointer only because that's what he said she was. She walked into his arms and he gently set her down on the driveway, where she stood looking drained of any emotion—not a single movement, not a minor clue to her feelings one way or the other.

I said nothing as I turned and led the way to the field. At the edge of the high grass she sat and looked a bit expectantly at her master who waved her on with a slight movement of one finger. She made a half-circle to get a feeling for whatever little breeze there was and began a comfortable trot toward a likely looking patch of heavy briers about 60 yards away. As she worked out in front of us I marveled at the way she eased through the grass. She had to be the smallest pointer I ever saw; almost pure white with a tiny lemon disc around one eye and so tiny that I could have easily imagined a porcelain dog placed here in the field for some bizarre photograph.

She had stopped on a rather classic point, a good 20 yards short of the briers.

"Would you like me to flush the bird or would you like to see her do it?" her handler asked me.

Almost speechless and still not convinced that I was looking at a real animal, I told him to have her flush. I immediately regretted the decision because I didn't think there was really a bird there and I doubted that she was actually hunting after being cooped up for Lord knows how long, and because I suddenly couldn't envision that tiny thing forcing her way into the heavy brambles. But before I could say anything she had been silently waved on and in a few seconds a crackling rooster came soaring out, followed for a few feet by the dog who looked hardly any bigger than the cock bird. She immediately stopped and marked the flight of the bird.

For the next hour I watched as unforgettable an exhibition of dog work as I will ever be privileged to see. She flushed on command and marked every bird's flight. When one of us chose to do the flushing she stood as still as alabaster and even rolled her eyes rather than turn her head any more than was absolutely necessary. When we had finished working the cover the Southerner patted his hand on his left thigh and she heeled instantly and sat waiting our pleasure—only her eyes were different now and the small veins in her legs were pumping with excitement, the only betrayal of emotion that she had revealed. She had the remoteness of a surgeon who is competent beyond any need for assurance.

"Very nice," I said. "Have you ever worked her on pheasant before?"

"I don't gun pheasant," he said, in a tone of voice that rebuked me for even having asked.

Back at the truck he patted the tailgate once, and she flew up on the deck and vanished into the kennel. Then he began his sales pitch, every word of which I fully believed.

"That's a little dog, I know, but one of the smartest and best I ever trained. She'll work your woodcock, your grouse, your pheasant. She'll retrieve dove and you'll never lose a one." And, as a clincher, he added, "She don't eat too much, either."

"What's her name?" I asked him.

"She don't have a name," he answered. "I just trained her for the fun of it and because it was so easy I figured that when I sold her, you could name her. I don't talk to dogs anyway . . . it puts the birds down if you make too much noise."

"I don't need a dog," I told him, pointing to my kennel where four Labradors were barking their untrained heads off.

"You don't have a bird dog," he said, "and you won't see one like this one for a long time—maybe never."

I told him I couldn't afford to buy or keep another bird dog.

"You didn't ask how much I want for her. Just guess."

I hate this kind of buyer-seller guessing because I'm always wrong and this time would be no exception. I had a . . . good idea what this dog was worth—"no papers" included. (He had no use for papers and I knew better than to ask; we'd been through that before.)

"It's the end of the season," I said, "and I don't want to board a dog and fool with one for a year before I can hunt. I travel a lot and won't be able to take her along."

"The people you hunt with ain't ever seen a better dog," he said.

"I couldn't take that dog as a gift," I told him, and then quickly added that wasn't really how I meant it.

"Well, if it was your dog what would you sell it for?" he asked me.

I thought that if that were my dog it wouldn't be for sale at any price . . . and just told him that if I had it, it wouldn't be for sale. His face softened and he smiled a little and said that he'd sell her for $350 and I could turn around and sell her for twice that—which was true.

"I won't bargain. I need that much and you're the first per-

son I asked. I'll get her sold and you know it . . . I just thought
I'd give you the chance to own a really good dog for a change."
(This he said with a rolling of the eyes at the Labradors trying
to climb the wire.)

As I stood there, the little white pointer stuck her nose out
of the kennel as though she was taking part in the conversation. Her head turned from him to me and I had to look away. I
really couldn't afford another dog, either in time or money. I
was field-trialing two of the Labs and that was stretching me
beyond reason as it was. Yet I wanted that little dog at that
moment as much as I'd ever wanted almost anything I can remember. And I believe as much as I believe in anything that
she wanted to stay there with me, too. I had to walk away from
the truck where I wouldn't see her. So I . . . motioned for him to
come sit with me at the back of the house.

As he went chatting on, suspecting my weakness, I couldn't
help but wonder what there was in him that created such absolutely amazing bird dogs. I couldn't imagine him either being
kind or violent in his training. I knew he was part Indian, and
that part was always up front: unemotional, pragmatic, stolid;
the classic hunter, as deadly quiet as a snake or a falcon. His
way with any animal—including me, had some undefinable
magic, and it made me slightly uneasy thinking about it.

I . . . turned to him and said, "I just can't do it now."

He said nothing; just stared at me with empty eyes and
flushed me out.

Almost unwillingly I added, "But if you don't sell her in a
week or so call me and I'll take her at your price."

He never answered me, just got in his truck and drove off.
As the pickup went down the lane, the kennel door flapping
open, the little white pointer's head came out and she looked

at me in a way that still causes me pain to think about. I know now that if she'd jumped out and come to me I'd have never let her go. In a way I never have. For over a month I alerted the family every day for his phone call which I never really expected and, of course, he never would have made.

I named her Daisy, in my imagination, after a dog I'd had too briefly some time before. And if I hunted with you tomorrow and saw a little white and lemon pointer I'd have to go over to see her, as I have always done since with every dog that remotely resembled her.

Call me what you will: stubborn, foolish or stupid and I'll agree with you. It's only right that I pay for it every time I see a Carolina pickup, every time I see a distant flash of white in a bird field . . . every time I daydream of what might have been or see a white and yellow flower in a meadow in the spring.

from TEARS & LAUGHTER

My Angel With Fur

PAMELA SANTI MEUNIER

I grew up with dogs as a child and preferred their company to that of most humans. Dogs weren't complicated. You could count on them. In those turbulent years growing up, it was the steadfast, unconditional love of my dog, Tara, that kept me going. Losing her was like having my favorite color suddenly erased from the face of the earth, never to be seen again. My memory strained to remember the joy of her presence, but with nothing to compare it to, it eventually was lost in the gray bleakness of my grief.

My parents died not long after Tara. In fact, it was one loss after another until I found myself with no family to speak of and no more pets to share my home. I devoted my time to building a career, traveling, and trying to find Mr. Right. At a very young age, I was determined that my life was not going to be a wasted one. I wanted to see the world, have adventures, and experience as much as I could. By the time I was 30, I was ready to settle down. I had moved to the Berkshires in Massachusetts, to a small farm located twenty-seven miles from the nearest market. A farm meant animals, flowers, fresh grown vegetables, and best of all, a dog! My dream was to find a purebred Golden Retriever, preferably a female, so I could raise puppies. Before long the neighbors up the street announced that their Goldens had mated and, knowing my dream, offered me the pick of the litter. Few things have given me more delight than fat, fluffy puppies. I was overjoyed. After many years of struggling through life's hardships, it felt as if all my dreams were coming true.

The longest weeks of my life were spent that summer waiting for Cleo's litter to be born. When her due week finally came, I rushed home from work each night and went straight up to their house to see if the puppies had arrived. Cleo got fatter and fatter, and looked as if she would burst if she had to wait one more minute. But each day would pass and still nothing. Einstein was right. Time is relative. It has certainly been my experience that the things you want most take forever to arrive, and the things you dread are here in a flash.

The call came early one morning while I was stumbling around the kitchen making coffee. Cleo had given birth to eleven healthy, hungry puppies. I dropped everything and ran up the street. What a sight! They were all curled around each other like caramel taffy while Cleo sat on guard, trying not to nod off from exhaustion. I sat on the floor next to the whelping box and watched them whimper and squirm, sleeping in the safety of their mother's warmth. Susie, Cleo's owner, was kind enough to bring me a cup of coffee. She had been up all night with the delivery but, like me, was too excited to go to bed. We sat on the floor in the mud room and watched the miracle of newborn life.

I cannot be certain if my eyes were drawn to one particular puppy, or if this puppy drew my gaze to her. Nevertheless, once I saw her and stroked her little back, I knew she was the one. "That is my puppy. That is the one I want." Susie looked at me quizzically and said, "They were just born. You have weeks to go before you need to make a decision. Why not wait until they are about a month old when their personalities will begin to emerge?" Her words fell on deaf ears. This was my puppy, the one that I had waited for since Tara's death almost twenty years before. I gently placed my large hand on her small back and told her she was my girl, that I would visit her every day until it was time to come home with me. She was only three hours old when we found each other. I know Susie did not take me seriously and assumed that when the time came, I would pick the cutest puppy and that would be it. But I never did change my mind. I couldn't because the decision wasn't actually made by me. It was merely shown to me. She was my girl and there would be no parting us from that moment on.

Ripe pumpkins and a few gourds were all that was left of the summer garden when Tosha came home with me. The fall air held a particular bite to it that signaled the onset of winter. Winters are long in the Berkshire's, but this winter I would have my puppy to keep me company. Tosha was a great companion because her presence filled the room. When Tosha was inside, all attention was focused on her. Even friends who weren't particularly fond of animals loved her. She soon acquired a following of admirers who would take her camping, hiking, swimming, and sledding. She was happy and in turn, made everyone around her happy. This was a gift I thought all Goldens possess, and to a certain extent, I think this is true. But Tosha had something more, and that "something" was revealed to me increasingly over the years.

Tosha's enthusiasm taught me to soak up the essence of each moment, to not hold back, or postpone for later, the joy awaiting our reunions. Her sphinx-like patience and groundedness demonstrated a level of trust and acceptance that I sorely lacked. The most important quality, I was privileged to witness over the fourteen years we spent together, was a loving tenderness so sweet that I have come to regard it as angelic. There are countless heartwarming examples, but the one that comes to mind is a story I was blessed to witness, but almost didn't.

Tosha and I lived with two cats, Sufi and Niki. It was a beautiful spring day, the animals were outside in the yard and I was preparing lunch. All of a sudden, I heard an ungodly screech, and a few moments later, the sound of cats howling and scampering off into the woods. I rushed to the window to see what had happened. To my horror, the cats had trapped and killed a young baby rabbit. Outraged, Tosha chased the cats from their prey. Ever so gently, she picked up the limp, little bunny in her mouth and carried it across the yard to the edge of the woods. There, she gently placed the bunny on the ground and dug a deep hole. With slow, methodical care, she placed the rabbit in the hole and proceeded to cover it up. Tosha then stood by the grave as if to say a prayer and a final good-bye. After a while she turned away, and went back to her favorite spot in the shade for her nap.

I stood in awe at what I had witnessed. It was then that I began to think of Tosha as my angel with fur.

Our journey together was filled with painful challenges as well as joys. I am reminded of the time when I was very ill with female problems and the news that I would not be able to bear children cut through me like a knife. My husband and I separated and many friends proved not to be friends, but Tosha always stayed close and steadfast. I feel in my heart that she was sent so that I could get through those painful years. It has been said that angels appear and answer our prayers when we remember to ask for their help. I believe, without a doubt, that she was sent as my answer.

The ironic part of our relationship is that even when I appeared to be helping her, in retrospect, I came to understand that she was truly helping me. A perfect illustration of this was when Tosha was pregnant. When I discovered that I was sterile, I transferred all of my maternal instincts to her and the prospect of having a litter of puppies. I found her the perfect mate, and when she was in heat, I bred them. She was young and had excellent papers, as did the sire, and everyone excitedly awaited the blessed event. I did everything by the book: made the perfect whelping box, saved lots of newspapers, and fed her beef liver, egg and rice omelets. Nothing was too much trouble for her and her puppies. She was in "hog heaven," or should I say, "dog heaven." She was as big as a house when her due date arrived. Up until then, Tosha was frisky and appeared in good health.

We were in the kitchen and I was making my morning coffee when suddenly Tosha stood up and her water broke. The kitchen floor flooded with a foul-smelling green liquid. For the first time in her life, Tosha looked scared. When I called the vet and described the situation, he became very alarmed. He asked me to carefully put her in the car and get to his office as fast as I could. Tosha was very large. Even before her pregnancy, she weighed 82 pounds of solid muscle. Now she must have weighed over 100 pounds. How could I possibly lift her into the car? I took a few deep breaths, said a prayer, and looking Tosha right in the eye, I told her no matter how hard or painful it was, she had to help me do this. Her courageous spirit never let me down, and it did not then. It almost killed her, but she got into the car.

The vet explained that her entire litter of eleven puppies was dead. He had to surgically remove the sack very carefully because if it burst before he could get it out, she would die. He told me gravely that she only had a slim chance of surviving, and that he would do his best.

The operation took six hours. It seemed more like six days as I sat in the waiting room, praying she would not be taken from me. I had come to rely on her presence. She was my anchor and my closest friend.

Much to the vet's amazement, she pulled through. The long operation left her slightly brain-damaged and sterile, but I didn't care. I had my girl back and that was all that mattered. I was able to bring Tosha home in about a week. I expected her to be the same as she had been before, but she was not. Her head hung low. She didn't want to go for a walk or even take a swim. No matter what I did, I could not cheer her up. I finally called the vet and told him about her behavior. I wasn't sure if this was the brain-damage that he had talked about. He assured me she was simply depressed, that maybe if I went to the store and bought a stuffed animal to substitute for her lost litter, she might snap out of it. I was willing to try, although I couldn't imagine it actually working.

It was Easter and the only animals in the store were bunnies. I hoped it wouldn't matter that it wasn't a puppy. I chose a big white one with long ears. Tosha always greeted me at the door, but this time was different. After weeks of being listless and deeply depressed, Tosha took one look at the Easter bunny, gleefully grabbed it out of my hand, and pranced off with it to her bed in a tail-wagging frenzy. She had become her happy, loving self again, and in that instant, her joy returned. She had a baby to love and care for, and that was all she wanted. Since then, I have given her a "baby" every Christmas, and every one of them is greeted warmly like that first time.

She loves, cares for, and grooms it, and when company comes over, she proudly displays it to all the guests. When I discovered I would never have children, I experienced a tremendous loss. I felt barren and without purpose. Interestingly, it was Tosha who supported me most through that painful time, and then, ironically, she went through it herself. She taught me a most valuable lesson; to mourn what is lost, but to love and cherish what I have.

Tosha and I carried on with our lives and I wish I could say that after her loss and mine, life went on smoothly, but that was not the case. Several years passed and I began to notice a slight shift in Tosha's energy level. It was subtle at first, but became steadily more pronounced. One morning, she did not want to go for her walk. Instead, she just looked at me as if to say, "I am too tired. Please don't make me go." I took her to the vet to determine what was wrong, but he felt that without extensive tests and some blood work, a diagnosis was not possible. Over the years, Tosha and I developed a strong communication. She didn't "speak" to me often, but when she did it was loud, clear, and unmistakable. This was one of those times. Tosha did not want to go through any tests.

Years before when I was sick with endometriosis, I had seen a healer and an herbalist who had been helpful and supportive. I thought if anyone could help Tosha, she could. Her diagnosis was almost immediate, and it confirmed my worst suspicions. Tosha had leukemia. The healer suggested drastic treatment, which involved giving Tosha a poisonous herb. She said it would either kill the cancer or kill her. In her opinion, it was Tosha's only hope.

At first I was vehemently against it. I loved her too much to take the chance that I could actually be poisoning her. I was so bonded with Tosha that the thought of losing her made me collapse in tears. I did not feel strong enough to take this course of action. I asked God to give me the courage to do what was best for her, regardless of how I felt. I asked Tosha what she wanted me to do. I felt her say in her sweet and simple way, "There is happiness in death, and there is happiness in life, but there is no happiness in this sickness. Don't hold onto me." Tearfully, I took in her words and her wisdom. I went to bed knowing that the next morning, I would let her treatment begin. Letting go of those I love has been a big part of my life's learning. In that day's sorrow, I was reminded once again that I do not own anything, not even myself, and that it is all on loan from God.

In my dreams that night, I had the most beautiful vision. Tosha was sleeping in her favorite, shady spot outside the door to my office and an angel appeared overhead. The angel circled the rooftop several times, and then floated down and effortlessly picked Tosha's spirit up and off they both flew into the clouds. Tosha's golden body remained looking peacefully asleep on the warm grass. This vision of Tosha's death gave me a sense of peace. It was so vivid that, upon waking, I took out my easel and painted it. The painting took several hours, and when it was complete, I gave Tosha her first dose of medicine. As I stirred it into her food, I told her that no matter what happened she was the most precious thing in all the world to me, a gift from God. I would not, however, let my needs infringe upon her freedom in any way. She was free to go, if it was her time. I would not hold her back.

The treatment plan took six weeks. It consisted of daily hands-on healing treatments which I administered twice a day. Those six weeks were long and arduous. One day she would appear to get better, only to relapse on the next. I had no idea what would happen. I only knew that during this period, I had learned something that previously I had only experienced on the surface. I knew unconditional love, the kind that has no expectation and needs no recognition. It is loving for the pure joy of loving, a complete act that needs nothing. I finally began to experience what a great teacher of mine once said, "Love is the reward for loving." I finally understood what she meant.

Tosha miraculously survived and recovered fully. Once again she could run, swim and eat all of her dinner. I have known joy because of Tosha and I have know unconditional love. Her sweetness eludes description, but the effects are clearly seen on anyone who has come in contact with her.

Tosha is now fourteen years old. Her hips are riddled with arthritis and a stroke has left her blind in one eye. She is leaving me slowly, like a summer sunset that spreads colors across the sky when the sun is still high in the west. Each day I say good-bye, not knowing if it will be our last, but I have kept my promise to her. I will not hold her. She knows she is loved, and free to go.

All that is left to say is, "Dear friend, you are all that is fine, good, and loving in this world. God must be very proud of you. You have done your job well. No one could have done better. Bless you, old girl."

God sent me an angel, an angel with fur, and I have been lifted up by it.

from ANGELS WITH FUR

The Loving Cat Who Kept His Word

LeGRAND DAY

I live in an "old folks" home with my best friend and room-mate, Elijah. Now, Elijah is a gray-striped tabby cat. He is only 3 years old. I am 63 and, I thought, a member of a superior species. However, we compete daily to see who is really running the place.

My former neighbor, Helen, just loved Elijah. She came by at least twice a day to visit him. Being the affectionate gentleman cat he is, Elijah reveled in her attention.

Helen was always ready to cat-sit whenever I was away for a few days.

The other residents thought Helen was different. True, she was slightly mentally challenged, had never married, had very few friends and no apparent relatives, and was always ready to argue. But she loved animals, especially my pal, Elijah.

You could say, Helen and I were somehow bonded by our mutual love for my cat.

When Helen became extremely ill, she was sent across the street to a board-and-care facility to die.

Three weeks later, I discovered she had no visitors in the

weeks she had been there. I promptly put Elijah in his cat carrier and took him over to visit her.

I very gently set him on the foot of her bed and opened the
carrier door. Being in a strange, new place, he cautiously peeked
outside. As soon as Elijah heard Helen's voice, he ran across
the bed to her. And her welcome was as heartfelt as always.

Elijah and I visited Helen about three or four times a week.
The head nurse asked if I would take him to visit other animal-
loving patients. I became a volunteer and loved seeing the dis-
mal faces brighten into smiles whenever I knocked on a door
and said, "Elijah is here to see you!"

I know my cat enjoyed all the extra attention. I always had
a hard time getting him back into his cat carrier.

Of course, we did spend most of our time with Helen. She
would always end the visits by holding Elijah close to her and
say to him, "Elijah, my dear friend, I don't want to die alone. . . .
Will you please be with me when I go?" He would always answer her with a wagging tail and a long, loving purr.

I got the call at 11:30 on a warm night. Helen was calling
for Elijah. We hurried over there. Our friend did not look good,
but a sweet smile came over her tired face when she saw
Elijah. She held out her arms for him.

They did their usual loving routine for the last time. Then
Helen's tired arms slowly slipped away from around Elijah. Her
eyes closed, and she just went away. Elijah smelled her forehead, cheeks, nose, and lips for a few moments. He gave a sad
little meow as if to say, "Goodbye my friend." He looked at me
for a moment, and then with no persuasion from me, Elijah
slowly walked back to his cat carrier.

Elijah's friend Helen did not die alone.

from HEART SONGS FOR ANIMAL LOVERS

For the Love of Snowball

NANCY B. GIBBS

On a freezing Christmas Eve, a little ball of fur entered my life. My most wanted Christmas wish had come true. My sweet husband, all excited, brought home the cutest Spitz puppy I had ever seen. "Snowball" became her name. She was white as snow, and since the weather was so cold the name seemed very fitting.

She took to me immediately and began untying my shoestrings while playing endlessly. The patter of her little feet and the scratching of her toenails filled our home with love and laughter.

As Christmas Eve progressed, I noticed that her eyes were turning red while she coughed and sneezed. I immediately called the pet store. They offered to refund our money or to exchange her for another puppy.

"No way," I said. "I already love her." We took a trip to the veterinarian's office instead. He diagnosed her with distemper and further stated that she probably wouldn't make it through the night. He suggested that the humane thing would be to put her to sleep.

With tears streaming down my face, I chose to give her

a chance and took her back home. I loved her too much to let her die or to return her, even if I could exchange her for a healthy puppy. All through that Christmas Eve, I nursed Snowball. I cuddled her, fed her chicken soup, prayed for her, but mostly loved her. She wouldn't take her eyes off me, and there was so much love in those big, brown eyes. A wonderful friendship was formed that night.

On Christmas Day, she seemed to have made some improvement, but was still very sick. At times, I questioned whether I was helping her or hurting her by attempting to keep her alive. But each time that I looked into her eyes, my heart melted. I realized on Christmas afternoon, that the gift my husband had given me was much more than a ball of fur, it was a gift of true love, given by a very sick puppy. Through the love of Snowball, I learned a great deal about compassion and commitment. If there was anything that could be done for her, I was determined to do it.

The chicken soup, coupled with hope, worked wonders. Over the next few days, she got better and began playing again. I knew deep down in my heart that she was going to make it and that the two of us would become the best of friends.

Several years later, my life as a city girl took a dramatic change when our family moved to the country. As I was walking across my backyard one afternoon, Snowball began frantically barking from her pen. She was growling, snarling, and jumping, as if she were trying to warn me of an upcoming danger. Since this was so unlike her, I knew that something was wrong.

I stopped walking and turned to speak to her. Then I saw something move in front of me. There was a five-foot-long rattlesnake, coiled up, ready to strike. If I had taken one more step, I would have been bitten. Considering the size of the snake and the distance to the hospital, I probably would not have lived. I slowly backed away, realizing that Snowball had saved my life. She had returned the favor from many years earlier.

Over the past twelve years, Snowball has survived many illnesses. Besides the distemper as a puppy, she has had spinal meningitis and heartworms twice. She has surprised both the vet and me many times, by pulling through. Her determination to live is as great as her desire to love.

Today, Snowball cannot see or hear very well, but she never fails to greet me when I come home from work each day. She stands at the fence and wags her tail until I tell her that I love her. She then runs and plays, knowing for sure that the relationship we formed many years ago is just as strong as it was then.

The fact that both Snowball and I are still alive today is nothing less than a miracle. I am convinced that God places people and pets together for a reason. People need to be loved unconditionally. Pets need to be cared for and taken care of, as well. When a relationship is formed between the two, there's nothing that one will not do for the other.

For the love of Snowball, I gave up sleep one Christmas Eve, but I gained so much more over the years to follow. There is no doubt that if Snowball could have got out of the pen the day I faced that snake, she would have. She would have protected me even if it had cost her life. Snowball has taught me some of the greatest lessons I've ever learned. She taught me about the unconditional love, compassion and devotion that a pet can give.

Nursery Duty

NIKI ANDERSON

Seventeen-year-old Rob Mann has no memory of life without Midnite, his female cat of equal age. One day, when Rob was a mere toddler, the black cat with two white whiskers followed him and his mother, Debbie, home from the bus stop. Day after day Midnite faithfully trailed behind Rob, until finally, on a cold and windy day, Debbie pitied the cat and gave her a bowl of food. When she refused to leave the doorstep Debbie finally let her indoors. Within the hour, Midnite declared herself mistress of the household by napping in the center of Debbie's bed.

Rob was a likely candidate for a cat in need of a good owner. His love of animals was evident even as a young child. At the age of four, he joined the 4-H club, and would continue on to serve as vice-president in his teens. The Berrien County 4-H Extension Office awarded the high school senior a county medal for his achievements in working with animals.

Most valuable to Rob is Midnite's lifelong companionship. "She's a real loving animal—a good old cat," said Rob. "We're pretty close, Midnite and me. She proved it when we moved from St. Joseph to Eau Claire. Midnite was about twelve years old. To get her used to the new area, we left her in Eau Claire with my grandma for a few days before we moved there. Three days later Grandma called and said Midnite was gone. The Humane Society picked her up in Benton Harbor, only three miles from our home in St. Joseph. She'd traveled twelve miles in her attempt to return to us. She was in good shape, though. We were sure glad to see each other."

After Midnite's adoption by the Manns, she established herself as guardian and caretaker of the young animals who are nurtured at the Mann's five-acre mini-farm in Eau Claire. "She's always got babies to care for," said Rob, "and has always commanded the respect of the animals we've owned."

Rob's 4-H projects often require a newborn animal of various species. Debbie willingly converts her master bathroom into a nursery. Ducklings and baby geese splash in the whirlpool bathtub while Midnite sits on the edge of the tub supervising their first attempts at swimming.

One year Rob raised a turkey for the small animal auction at the fair. He placed the caged turkey in the bathroom under a heat lamp. Midnite tended it for over a month. Whenever it chirped, Midnite looked anxious and led Rob or Debbie to the bathroom. Often, there was a genuine need like replenishment of food. "Midnite would circle the cage and appear relieved that we responded," said Debbie.

One of Midnite's favorite charges was a Nubian goat. Rob put the ten-day-old goat in his bedroom inside a portable dog kennel. During the day, Midnite watched, slept, and groomed beside the cage. The little goat had to be fed around the clock. Midnite maintained a clean environment for him by licking up drops of spilled formula after feedings. Though Midnite seldom goes outside, when the goat wanted out, she followed behind and waited on the front steps until he returned, then followed him back to the kennel.

For several years the Manns had a feisty teacup poodle named Pierre. He got along with no one but Midnite, probably because Midnite made it clear that she was the boss. They became soul mates. Midnite let Pierre sleep with her in the cozy oval cat bed. It was an unlikely sight, the tiny but grown dog sleeping with a cat three times its size.

Midnite's gifts of nurturing and devotion have paid a return in personal acclaim. She has placed in the Berrien County Youth Fair competition for several years, in 1997 as Reserve Champion Cat Overall and as Grand Champion short hair. In 1998 she was awarded Grand Champion Overall. When the nearby town of Cassopolis, Michigan, hosted a two-day event honoring the inventor of cat litter, Midnite reigned over the festival as the female feline sovereign and was recognized with a Lifetime Achievement award as the oldest competitor. But the Manns contend Midnite's most prestigious achievement is her attitude toward all the pets in their home whom she could have viewed as rivals rather than as youngsters in need of her care.

Perhaps Midnite has never forgotten how scary it was when she was a homeless cat. When the Manns adopted her, she was less than a year old and obviously lost. Could it be that she remembers what it was like to be young and to yearn for a caregiver? Maybe that's why she has a heart for all the chicks, ducklings, puppies, and goats she has nannied over the years.

Feeling compassion for those who have endured misfortunes similar to our own is a powerful way to salvage a negative experience. Midnite went a step further. She turned her compassion into kind action by nurturing the young lives of other animals.

from INSPUR-R-RATIONAL STORIES FOR CAT LOVERS

Murphy

ALISON PFAELZER

$\mathcal{H}$e came to me when he was two months old. A good friend knew that I had been thinking of getting a dog. So one day at work she made a phone call, and 10 minutes later a puppy was placed in my arms—it was love at first sight! I named him Murphy.

Murphy was very small when I got him. He was mostly white with a black-and-brown masked face, and he had three large black spots on his body. I used to call him my little speckled pup.

Murphy and I were together 10 years. I have never been married and have no other children (human or otherwise), so he was everything to me. He was there to laugh with me during the good times (he could really smile) and was there to console me during the bad. There was one point in my life when I had orthopedic surgery that went bad, and I almost lost my foot. For five long months, I was dependent on crutches and had to sleep on the couch. Murphy seemed to understand and know just what to do. He would always "ask" before he jumped up to lie next to me. And though he loved to go out frequently, when he realized that it was hard for me to get to the door, he held back and waited. He would sleep on the couch with me every night. But when my foot hurt and I'd ask him to get down, he would lie, uncomplaining, on the floor beside me. I kept a journal during this hard time, and as I read through it, I see that I wrote—over and over again—"Thank God for Murphy; I don't know what I would ever do without him."

We moved several times, and as hard as it was for me every time, Murphy was always there to be my friend when I didn't have any. We'd chase each other around the house, play tug, and go for long walks. When the men in my life left, there Murphy was, licking my ear and letting me know that he still loved me and that everything would be fine because he was there. I would talk to him constantly, tell him whatever I was thinking or feeling, and he would listen to my every word. I knew he understood. And just knowing that Murphy was always there for me with his unconditional love was enough to get me through anything.

He had so much character. I loved his different expressions, especially the quizzical way he cocked his head and looked at me with his beautiful brown eyes. And he had this big ol' grin that always made me smile. It wasn't your regular dog grin, it was an ear-to-ear people smile! I used to call him my little Pinocchio because I believed he wanted to be a real boy. If I had been gone for too long (to his way of thinking) or leaving again, man, would I get cussed out! He didn't bark; it was more of a jabbering thing. He'd snap his teeth together as if to say, "Hey, you're not spending enough time at home." I would always assure him that I'd be back later to play.

When I was home and Murphy got bored, he would go to a piece of furniture and scratch it with his paw, then he'd look at me and snap those darn teeth together. If I didn't pay any attention, he'd move on to another piece of furniture—from a chair, to the coffee table, to the stereo. He knew this made me angry and wouldn't quit until I paid attention to him.

Every time I put on my shoes, Murphy would bound to the door. When I'd tell him that he could come with me, he would nip at my feet all the way to the car as if to say, "Hurry up, let's go!" He loved to go anywhere with me. His collar now hangs on my rearview mirror so that he gets to go everywhere with me.

Over the years, Murphy had his share of ear infections and stitches, but, otherwise, he seemed healthy. Then one weekend that all changed. Without warning he had several "attacks" that caused him to hunch his back while sitting, pant frantically, and drool. I rushed him to the animal hospital.

On Monday morning, I found out that Murphy was full of cancer. It was so bad that they didn't even bother to remove any of it, and they couldn't tell me whether he would live a day or a month.

When I went to pick him up the following day, I was unsure of what I would see or what I would do. When the vet opened his cage, Murphy ran to the front door, scratched on it, and looked up at me as if to say, "Well, let's go home!" He seemed like his old self. I was suddenly filled with hope, but it was short-lived. After only a few hours, he was again in a lot of pain. I had heard that cancer patients sometimes get one more burst of energy before they go. I think Murphy knew how sick he was and wanted to be at home. But by that afternoon, I knew what I had to do. I kept saying to him, "You're going to make me do it today, aren't you?" It was his 10th birthday.

He was so very tired but would not sleep. He just sat there trying to keep himself propped up with his front legs, staring at me or out the window. It seemed that he was hanging on just for me—and *I* couldn't let go. I struggled with the thought of losing him but could not watch him suffer anymore. I called the vet. The vet was extremely nice and came to our house. It was done on our bed in "mama's loving arms." That's exactly what I told him as I carried him to his grave. He is now buried outside my bedroom window, the window he stared out of during his last hours. It's where I think he wanted to be.

As I look back, I wonder why I never knew he was that sick. Maybe the love we had between us was, in some way, a type of medicine. The cancer must have been there for a long time, but he never showed any signs of it. I don't know if he was hiding it from me, but I guess I'll never know.

What I do know is that he will always be with me. A few days after he died, I was walking down the hall, and I smelled him. I immediately cried because I knew he was there. I still "see" him walking up to me, wagging that stub tail of his, sticking his nose up so I will bend down and kiss him. As strange as this might sound (I have questioned my own sanity), I hear him in this little boy's voice, "Mama, I'm still here. I love you, I miss you, too." And when I go to sleep at night, I feel him curled up in the crook of my knees. It's funny, I still talk to him all the time and feel as if he hears me.

All the years we were together, I kept telling him, "Someday we'll have our very own house in the country." We moved to our new house in the country not quite two months before he died. I can't help but feel that Murphy waited for me to be happy and in a safe place before letting go. I still feel his presence and believe I always will. We were such a part of each other's lives that I don't think it could be any other way. I know for certain that I wouldn't want it to be.

from HEART SONGS FOR ANIMAL LOVERS

Memories

KATHY BETH McDONALD

$\mathcal{T}$he lucky ones lived in the past. Some were confined with restraints for their own safety. Others shuffled around aimlessly, resigned to spending the rest of their days in an indigent-care nursing home. Some were visited by family members on weekends and holidays. A few were all alone, having outlived their children, or been abandoned by them. They all longed for a loving touch.

Two-year-old Heather had love to spare. My husband and I adopted her from the local Humane Society when she was eight months young. A Terrier-Spitz with a Pomeranian face, she delights in meeting people. She hops on legs made of springs, stretches out her arms, and gives little kisses to anyone who will accept them. I felt a trip to the nursing home was in order.

Heather was on her best behavior. Black lips in a perpetual grin, she made the rounds and greeted everyone. Hands, which spent most days folded in laps, stretched out to touch her. Faces lit with joy when she wiggled in greeting. Men chuckled and women laughed at her loving kisses.

When they saw her, she reminded them of happy times. They told stories about dogs who had accompanied them on their farm rounds and about pampered animal friends who learned to sit daintily on chairs covered with lace doilies.

One woman's reaction will forever be etched in my mind. She hugged my little dog to her, and began to cry. After awhile, I gently lifted Heather from the woman's grasp. I held the woman until there were no more tears. For a moment, we had all been touched by love.

from DOG TALES FOR THE HEART

Trusting Others

"Shared joy is double joy, and shared
sorrow is half-sorrow."

SWEDISH PROVERB

$\mathcal{A}$nimals often have good reasons not to rely on people, and yet they do. They seem to have the ability to forgive us our trespasses and to hope for something better. Fortunately it sometimes happens. And if it doesn't, our animal friends still won't give up on us.

They may very well be telling us how God loves us.

Nobody's Bird

ANNE WATKINS

"Don't try to pet the Amazon," the manager warned as I started to enter the bird room of my favorite pet store. "He's vicious! He's attacked all of us and drawn blood."

I peered through the screened wall at the ragged, dusty bird sitting quietly in a large cage. He glared back.

"His name is Pancho," she continued. "He's here on consignment but I don't think we'll ever be able to sell him. He's just too mean."

"I won't go near him," I promised.

Telling me to let her know if I needed anything, the manager went to wait on another customer. I stepped into the bird room and went to play with the baby umbrella cockatoo. Several of the cages were open, allowing the birds the freedom to come out and play if they chose. Pancho's cage was securely closed, but I steered clear of his area just the same. He was a pretty good sized bird—his head was about as big as a newborn puppy's and I knew that he could do serious damage with that nasty looking beak if I got close enough for him to reach between the bars and grab at me.

I had played with the fluffy white cockatoo for just a few minutes when a soft voice behind me said, "Hello."

I looked around but no one was there. I turned back to the cockatoo.

"Hello," came the voice again. Glancing around, I realized that it was coming from Pancho's cage! We made eye contact and he stepped a couple of inches along his perch toward me.

Glancing around to see if the manager was watching, I went over to the Amazon's big, square cage. It stood mid-chest high to me and I had to bend down to be at Pancho's eye level. He looked steadily back at me and reached his beak toward the bars. I carefully put a finger on one of the bars near his face. To my surprise, he didn't lunge toward me; instead he looked me right in the eye.

"Hello," I said.

Pancho slowly reached one foot out through the bars toward me. I touched his toe. When he didn't flinch away, I moved slowly up to touch the feathers on his leg, then his wing. Next I lightly massaged his shoulder. Then he sat very still as I cautiously slipped the tip of my finger through the bars and stroked his beak. From outside the bird room, I heard the manager say softly, "I don't believe this."

Without moving my eyes from Pancho's, I asked, "Has he ever let anyone get close to him?"

"No!" she replied. "He hates everybody."

I continued to caress the shy, bedraggled parrot while he sat quietly soaking up the attention. Occasionally, he made a soft little sound but not once did he become aggressive.

After awhile, I decided to visit some of the other birds. When I stepped away from the cage, Pancho let out a shriek that almost peeled the paint from the walls. I hurried back to him. He shut up immediately and reached his foot out toward me again.

I tried to leave several times and each time he let loose

heart wrenching cries. I asked the manager if maybe I reminded Pancho of somebody he had once loved. Not as far as she knew, she said. He was nobody's bird. I was touched by this lonely little soul's apparent trust of me, a total stranger.

Finally, I had to go home. I quickly stepped out of the building, trying not to hear the desperate screams echoing through the store.

When I returned a few days later, the manager met me at the door. She told me that Pancho had shrieked for ten minutes after I left him. "He really must like you," she added.

"Really?" I asked. "Do you think he'll remember me today?"

That question was answered as soon as I stepped into the bird room. Pancho spotted me and rushed toward me, cooing sounds of welcome all the while!

I spent an hour or so with him that day. Before I left, I repeated my name to him several times and was rewarded with a quiet imitation that amazed me.

The same scene from our previous visit was repeated when I had to leave. Trying to speak over Pancho's heartbroken screeches, I told the manager that I would be back later that week to look at him again, and that if the bird still liked me, I would put a deposit on him. I left with desperate Amazon screams ringing in my ears.

I walked in three days later to be told as soon as I entered the store, "He yelled your name all day yesterday!"

That was it. How could I not adopt a bird that had chosen me? I couldn't stand the thought of Pancho sitting alone in his cage, frightened and confused, for one day longer. I was honored and amazed that he had selected me out of all the people who passed through the store.

Pancho has been with me for many years now. The

"vicious" bird who had once attacked anyone who got within reach is now a "cuddle bird." He fluffs his whole body and rushes to me, head down, for petting. He will sit still as long as I will scratch his head, or rub his shoulder. He takes treats from me and loves to be misted with cool water. He is very vocal, and says several words and phrases. There is also his famous duck imitation, his operatic solo and his maniacal laugh. He is a wonderful bird!

Even after all these years, I am honored beyond imagination to know that this once sad, lonely little bird picked me. The love that glows in his sweet orange and black eyes when he looks at me melts my heart. He knew that we should be together. I'm glad he was able to get that message across to me!

Each Other's Keepers

JAIME JACOBS

I soloed for the first time at the age of nine. That is, I rode my bike all by myself to the pet store. I doggedly negotiated stop signs and brazened my way through traffic signals, and only got lost once. After all that, I think I must have absolutely swaggered into the shop once I arrived. I was there to buy bird food for my budgies, Sidney and Adelaide; what I walked out with was the heady sense of having accomplished not one, but two, feats of derring-do. Not only could I now be considered a Trailblazer, I was also a Dauntless Decisionmaker, for I had gone and bought myself a mouse! Without a permit! Intoxicated with newfound effrontery, I was sure I could convince my parents it was A Good Thing.

My parents did *not* think a mouse in the house was a good thing at all, considering we already shared our home with assorted dogs and cats. These two worthy species are purported to be predators of small things that scurry and, as my parents kept pointing out to my utter annoyance, mice are indeed small and their preferred mode of transportation is to scurry. I thought it was a paltry argument, one that couldn't stand up to my printed list of seventeen remarkable reasons why I should have a mouse.

Somehow, and to this day I don't understand it, I managed

to persuade them to let me keep the wee beast. It may, in a tiny way, have had to do with my magnanimous offer to let Mom name it, since she never seemed to prevail when it came to naming our other pets. Daddy's choices were the ones that always stuck, resulting in appellations like "Musty," "Dandruff," and "Rancid," for the unsuspecting dogs who never did understand why strangers snickered rudely upon meeting them. The only influence Mom had on naming anybody was to insist upon spelling our cockapoo's name the French way, which she decided was "Mildieu," because it looked so much classier than the more mundane "Mildew."

Poor Mom was still smarting over the fact that she'd had to compromise on the issue of what to name my baby brother, so maybe having exclusive rights to mouse nomenclature was what swayed her in my favor. Whatever their reasons, my parents let me keep the mouse, a little red-eyed tan female that Mom decreed should be called Lupe because it was a Spanish name, like Speedy Gonzalez. Even more amazingly, Mom drove me back to the pet store that same afternoon to get little Lupe a companion. I'm pretty sure I know why Mom didn't let me go back all by myself. (A decade later, my new husband would quickly learn to impose the same restriction.) Most mothers worry that their children might get lost or hurt; mine was terrified I'd come home with a Komodo dragon.

I loved Lupe but I positively adored the newer mouse, which Mom named Poco in keeping with the Spanish theme. For one thing, Poco was bursting with mousely pulchritude, her coat a flashy brown and white pinto that would make a quarter horse envious. For another, I was convinced she was a "Japanese waltzing mouse," for in spite of being immensely fat, she moved with an impudent paddle of her back feet that I have never seen repeated in any other mouse. I'm not certain that Japanese waltzing mice exist, but at the time it seemed a fittingly impressive title. I wasn't Poco's only admirer, either. Our cat, Alley, found her fascinating and had to be forcibly restrained from proving it. But Poco's truest swain was Mildieu the cockapoo. It was love at first sniff for both of them.

Mildieu was never happier than when providing bus service to his pair of mouse passengers. They belted themselves securely into his fluffy black and white fur while I took the three of them on guided tours of the neighborhood. At home, the mice could barrel race between Mildieu's legs, weaving in and out without fear of getting stepped on. Most importantly, they willingly received what is a dog's highest accolade—they let Mildieu lick them, which he did frequently, like a child licks postage stamps.

I kept a variety of mice over the next several years but none was as loved as Poco. My brother, my cousin, my dog, we all revered her. She'd been with me for almost four years when I was awakened one night by a soft, insistent whine somewhere in the dark. I saw a white wraith across my room, near the mouse cage, and my first thought was that the monster under the bed had at last made a physical manifestation. Then I realized in relief that the shroud and the noise were just Mildieu standing with his head under the cage blanket. He sounded worried, so I switched on the lamp to investigate.

Sadly, it turned out that Poco was gravely ill. She was huddled, shivering, in a corner and her normally glossy fur had the greasy, clumped look that sick animals get. It wasn't entirely a shock since I had dreamed about her death just the week before. Still, she had seemed perfectly well when I tucked the mice in for the night, and now she was suffering, panting, her plump sides pulsing in little jerky motions as she tried valiantly to breathe. I wanted to help her or at the very least just to hold her, but her cagemate, Rosa, was delicately bathing Poco's face and ears and I didn't like to disturb what surely looked like an act of animal compassion. Most scientists will say animals don't engage in altruism and that they don't grieve, but I believe I saw both that night.

Mildieu and I held a vigil by the light of my aquarium, I with icy knees and feet and he standing with his front paws on the table. I remember thinking my discomfort was only fitting at a death watch, and for all I know Mildieu felt the same way, gallantly maintaining his pose all through the night. The poor fellow whimpered quietly but continuously, only taking his eyes off Poco on occasion to lick away the tears coursing down my face. I was grateful because their saltiness had started to sting but I didn't like to wipe them away myself, each tear being a tribute to my dear, dying friend. After licking my face, Mildieu would gaze beseechingly at me, as if imploring me to do something, anything. In happier moments, that same expression showed on his face whenever I ate a hamburger in front of him. It was a very earnest look and very hard to resist on the best of days. It was even more heart-rending on this gloomiest of nights. However, all I could do for Mildieu in the end was open the cage door to let him nudge Poco with his nose. Perhaps he was assuring himself that the vitality truly had gone from her tiny body. After nudging her to no avail, he finally laid down in front of the cage and with an audible sigh, rested his head on his paws. For the first time during that long, difficult night Mildieu allowed his eyes to drift shut.

I wrapped Poco's body in pink pajama flannel and the next day laid her to rest under the ice plant outside my bedroom window. I wrote her name in my best pretend calligraphy on the memorial scroll where I wrote the names of every pet I'd ever lost. Poco joined Sidney and Adelaide and Lupe and many others, and many others would follow over the years, but I made sure to leave a space just below her name.

Later, in the days when I was fifteen and busier with peers than with pets, I nevertheless dug that scroll out of my sock drawer one terrible night and added Mildieu's name. Nestled above it was Poco's name, and I remembered the way she used to nestle in his silky fur, proof of something that continues to give me hope in a difficult world.

If two creatures born into natural enmity can rise above it to love each other, then some day, maybe some day, we humans can rise above our differences, too.

Cat, a Bird's Best Friend!

NIKI ANDERSON

Sharon never suspected a sundown stroll with her cat, Cleopatra, would one day involve a lifesaving interlude. The Siamese, nicknamed Cleo, is primarily an indoor cat, but enjoys a nightly walk with her owner through the field behind Sharon's home.

Cleo and Sharon often conclude their promenade by sitting on the hillside and watching the sunset. Their walks are seldom eventful. They simply share a time of quiet rest and outdoor scenery. But one spring evening was different from the rest.

As Sharon and Cleo ambled along, Cleo dashed toward a fence and peered down at something that captured her attention. She meowed repeatedly, excitedly. Sharon presumed Cleo had spotted an insect or a skittering mouse, so she made no effort to hurry toward her. When she reached Cleo, she had to look hard for the object that had aroused the cat's interest. She fumbled through some fallen leaves and then she saw it— a scrawny bunch of tiny wings and legs. She instantly recognized the species of baby bird. Its russet shade and dark stripes were the color and markings of the California quail, one of Sharon's favorites.

"I stood there looking with Cleo, neither of us knowing what to do next. Cleo made no attempt to harm the bird or even draw closer. She was restless and appeared as concerned as I. She meowed occasionally, but kept turning to me as if to say, 'Well, do something!'"

Sharon sat down on the grass and began talking aloud, glancing at Cleo as if she understood every word. "*Now* what should I do? If I touch the bird, the parent may reject it. But maybe it's abandoned. It's almost dark and getting chilly. The animals that roam here at night will probably find the bird if I don't move it."

After wrestling through her thoughts, she said, "C'mon Cleo, let's call a wildlife rescue group and ask for advice."

Sharon telephoned a volunteer who explained that California quail are ground-nesting birds. She was told the chick was likely deserted only because the parents had been driven away. "Unattended, the bird probably won't survive the night," warned the volunteer. "Can you bring it to me?"

"Oh yes, if you think you can help!" Sharon was hopeful and relieved.

She found a small box and lined it with crumpled paper. Armed with a flashlight she headed back to the field and lifted the hapless bird into the container. Her husband offered to drive them to the volunteer's home.

Upon examination, the bird was judged healthy. "It seems to be in pretty good shape. I'm caring for thirty other birds, but I'll gladly take one more," said the volunteer, as she rushed away to select appropriate food for the trembling quail. Sharon and her husband left the bird and drove home with a feeling of commendation.

Sharon later pondered the rare string of events—a cat had

led to the rescue and salvation of a bird—an extraordinary occurrence between predator and prey. Thanks to Cleo's keen smell and sharp eyesight, at least one bird in Santa Clara County has a feline for a best friend.

from INSPUR-R-RATIONAL STORIES FOR CAT LOVERS

Restoring Rosie

ALLEN M. SCHOEN, DVM, AND PAM PROCTOR

From the very beginning, I sensed there was something peculiar about the dog. She was only a year old, a German shepherd, little more than an adolescent. Instead of walking into my office proudly and confidently, as most shepherds do, this one ran in with her tail between her legs and cowered under a chair. The minute her owner opened his mouth to speak, the dog sank down even lower to the floor.

According to the owner, Max, a hulking construction worker with the biggest biceps I had ever seen, the dog was having bladder problems. "She wets all over the house," he said. "I tell her to stop, and she keeps wetting even more. I've tried swatting her. I've tried yelling. Nothing works. It's driving me crazy."

"Okay. Let's take a look at her," I said. And as I started to talk, the dog, whose name was Rosie, peeked out from under the chair and sniffed at my leg.

"No!" shouted Max. "Stay still!"

Rosie's eyes filled with fear and she immediately scrunched up as small as she could underneath the chair.

There was an arrogance and brutishness to Max's voice that jarred me. It didn't take much to suspect that the dog's wetting problems were probably behavioral, not physical. But to be certain, I had to run a number of routine tests. It was possible that Rosie had a congenital problem. A complete urinaly-sis and battery of blood tests would tell if her kidneys were functioning properly or if she had an infection.

A day later, her tests came back negative, and I was even more certain that Rosie's problem was psychologically in-duced. Although German shepherds can give the impression of being assertive, this one had been low in the dominance order in her litter, according to her family history. It was quite pos-sible that she was naturally submissive and easily cowed by the tone of her master's voice. As a result she had become what is known as a "passive wetter."

How could I tell Max the truth—that Rosie was cowering and urinating because she was intimidated by him? How could I tell him that for the dog to get well, *he* would have to change?

I told Max that all of Rosie's tests were normal and, finally, I said as delicately as I could, "It might be that she has a behav-ioral problem."

Max wasn't ready to hear anything that smacked of psy-chology. "My dog's not a wimp!" he said bluntly. Then he turned to Rosie, and said in an ominous tone, "You're not a wimp, are you?"

At the sound of Max's voice, Rosie's ears dropped back, and from the look of terror in her eyes, I could tell that if I hadn't been in the room she might have been in for a beating.

"There's another test she can take," I interjected quickly, trying to break the tension. "A special type of x-ray will show us if she has any defect in the connection of the bladder to the urethra. I'll have the results in a day or two. Bring her back then and we'll see what we can do."

Unfortunately for me—and for Rosie—her x-rays also proved normal. Now it was up to me to break the news to Max.

As I explained the situation to him, he looked back and forth between me and the dog as though there was some sort of conspiracy between us. "Medically, your dog is fine," I said. "But from what you've told me about Rosie's personality, it's clear she has a low self-image and needs to be handled more gently."

The scowl on Max's face told me I was venturing into forbidden territory. "I know it may be difficult," I continued, "but you're going to have to act softer and kinder toward Rosie. She seems to be getting the wrong message from your tone of voice. She takes it as disapproval. The only solution is to try to build up her self-image. It'll take a lot of work—but it can be done."

At that, Max rolled his eyes and shook his head. Clearly, a dog as sensitive as Rosie was not his idea of man's best friend.

He sat there for a few moments, bristling inside. Then he stood up abruptly and said, "I don't want a wimpy dog. You can have her." And with that, he turned on his heel and walked out.

Rosie didn't even bother to look up. She just lay there under a chair, head on her paws, until I knelt down and whispered for her to come out. I extended my hand and she stretched out her head and started sniffing.

I patted her on the chest rather than on the head, so I would not appear threatening, and wondered what to do next. I wasn't sorry to see Max go. Although the prospect of filling my hectic schedule with yet another demand didn't exactly thrill me, I was overjoyed to have rescued Rosie from the clutches of a man who only wanted a dog created in his own rough image.

The challenge I faced was to draw out the dog that was buried inside Rosie—the personality that had been beaten down by an abusive and overcontrolling master. It would be a daunting task, but I was determined to give it a try. To lift Rosie's self-esteem would take a limitless supply of patience and love. But I knew that I would have a helpmate—my golden retriever, Megan. During the day when I was at work, she would be able to provide the kindness and nurture that Rosie needed.

That night, I took Rosie home and started her on a crash course in canine confidence building. The minute I walked in the door, Megan bounded over and began to sniff Rosie all over and smother her with affectionate licks. Rosie didn't seem to know what to do. Her eyes darted back and forth nervously as she stood with her shoulders hunched up tight. But after a few minutes, when she realized Megan wasn't a threat, she began to relax. Her body loosened up and she even managed to muster up a few tentative sniffs in return.

Later on, to put the newcomer at ease, I played for a while with Megan and then made a few gentle overtures toward Rosie. I lay flat on my stomach in a nonthreatening pose, and averting my eyes, held out my hand in a gesture of friendship. I knew that if I looked her straight in the eyes that it could be interpreted as a challenge, increasing Rosie's anxiety level and thwarting my efforts to boost her ego.

So I waited. And waited. After what seemed like an eternity, Rosie slowly moved toward my hand and started sniffing. I didn't move a muscle. She kept sniffing, and gradually I was able to lift my hand and start to pet her. All the while, I whispered words of assurance. Megan, meanwhile, stood quietly at the side of the room observing this interaction with what seemed like approval.

The next night, it was more of the same. I played with Megan, hoping to impress on Rosie a model of warm, loving behavior between friends, then I stretched out on the floor and held out my hand to draw her in. Within a few days, I was able to sit cross-legged on the floor with Rosie next to me as I stroked her, whispering words of encouragement and love.

But the picture wasn't all perfect. Some nights I would come home from work exhausted and find that Rosie had urinated in various corners of the house. There were telltale signs in the bedroom, in the corner of the living room, and in the den. My heart would sink as I contemplated the work that lay ahead. Not only did I have a mess to clean up, I also had to face the fact that Rosie's recovery wouldn't happen overnight.

But I couldn't let on what I was feeling. If my voice, eyes, or body language betrayed any trace of disapproval, Rosie would pick up on it immediately. So while I was cringing inside at the smell of urine and the sight of the damp spots on my rug, I always managed to smile and sound upbeat.

"Hi, girls, I'm home!" I would call out enthusiastically. And Megan would rush over to greet me, followed by a hesitant Rosie. I reached down to pet one, then the other. Then I knelt on the floor and put my arms around them both, giving them a big hug.

What Rosie needed was love, not punishment, no matter how egregious her behavior. If I wanted this dog to become the healthy and happy creature she was meant to be, I had to cling to my faith that one day soon the positive reinforcement I was giving her would pay off.

Finally, I began to see that Rosie's confidence was growing in small ways. After she had been with me for almost a week, I took a chance and looked her straight in the eye when I held out my hand in greeting. Instead of holding back, she came forward to lick my hand in what was for her a supreme act of trust.

Gradually, her bouts of wetting tapered off, and after about two weeks there were no more episodes. And her physical control was a reflection of her newfound confidence. One night when I walked in the door and shouted hello, it was Rosie, not Megan, who was the first to meet me. She ran right over to me with her tail wagging and raised her head to be petted. Our eyes met, and I could see from her enthusiastic greeting that she was a new dog.

"Rosie, you're great!" I exclaimed, squatting down and nuzzling up close. "I'm so proud of you!"

About a month later, I sensed that Rosie was well enough to move on to another family. It couldn't be just any family, of course. If I were to give her up, it would have to be to people who were compassionate and caring, who understood the universal need of anyone—animal or human—for love and encouragement. I found such people in the Bertellis, a wonderful couple with two young children, who embraced Rosie as if she were a long lost member of the family. Their enthusiasm for her was infectious, and only a few minutes into the first visit, it was clear that Rosie had transferred her trust from me to them without any hesitation.

The children loved Rosie immediately, and when the older son threw a stick for her to retrieve, she raced out on the lawn, picked it up in her mouth, and proudly returned it to the boy amidst cheers and applause. To see her like this, with her head held high and her gait sure and steady, it was hard to imagine that only a few weeks before she had been cowering under a chair in my office.

from LOVE, MIRACLES, AND ANIMAL HEALING

The Revival

NANCY B. GIBBS

One Wednesday night our congregation at Tippettville Baptist Church joined another church's congregation to share in their revival service. When my husband and I pulled into the driveway leading to the church, we were surprised to see an empty parking lot. As we got closer, we saw two small dogs staring at us.

The country church was on a highway in the middle of nowhere. When we got out of the car, both puppies came running our way. The larger of the pups was matted and covered with sand spurs. The other one, a short-haired brown dog, was much cleaner. Both dogs were hungry and very thirsty. That day's temperature had hovered between ninety and ninety-five degrees.

We walked around to the back of the church building and found a faucet. When we turned it on, both dogs lapped up the water. The matted pup even stretched out in the water, cooling off his empty belly.

In a little while, some other members of our church arrived. We came to the conclusion that the services were to begin thirty minutes later than we had thought. That explained why nobody was there to greet us, except the two thrown-away puppies. That also gave me ample time to fall in love

131

with them. I found a couple of packages of Saltine crackers in my purse, and the dogs ate them as if they were starving to death. Apparently, someone put the hungry puppies in the parking lot, knowing that a revival would be held that night.

Taking both puppies home would have been impossible since we were already the proud owners of two other dogs. My husband, Roy, wasn't excited about taking even one of them, much less two. When Mrs. Wilma, one of our church members, arrived, she agreed to take the short-haired puppy if I would take the other one. I was so happy to know that both puppies would have a home and families to love them.

When it was time for the revival services to begin, I left the puppies and went inside to worship and praise the name of Jesus. During the prayer time, I silently asked God to let the puppies be outside at the conclusion of the service if it was meant for me to take the dirty, matted, thorny little puppy home.

During the service, one of the church members went outside and returned to his pew a few minutes later. At the conclusion of the meeting, he walked over to me. "I believe your dogs are gone now," he announced. "They weren't out there a little while ago."

I felt somewhat sad but also a little relieved. I hurried out the front door just to make sure. I was the first person to exit the building, and there sat both puppies looking up at me, wagging their tails and begging for love. Despite the sand spurs and grime, I picked up the matted puppy and held it close. As I did, the sand spurs pierced my hands. I could imagine how horribly they must have been hurting him.

"We're going home now, Benji," I whispered. He looked up at me and licked my face. Mrs. Wilma picked up her new puppy and hugged it tightly. Family ties were formed immediately.

The revival service that night was spiritually uplifting. And when we arrived home, Benji was revived physically with a good dinner. The next day, I took him to the veterinarian for a check-up and bath. When he returned home, he was greeted with presents bought by my husband (who is now very happy to have him): bones, pull-toys and balls. While he likes his toys, he's happiest when we hold him and simply love him. Puppies know what are the most important things in life. Apparently Benji was just as hungry for love as he was for physical nourishment.

Benji wasn't the prettiest dog I had ever seen when I first laid eyes on him, but I looked beyond the matted fur and saw the hunger to love and be loved written on his dirty face. He helped me to understand a little more about God's love for all of us, and he was beautiful.

Rusty

KAREN DERRICO

$\mathcal{D}$ay after day, for nearly ten years, Rusty waited with a hopeful look in his eyes each time someone approached his cage at the shelter. He was getting old, almost sixteen. His rust-colored coat had become dull and arthritis was beginning to take its toll. The chances of someone adopting a dog that age are pretty slim, but the Animal Protection League in South Carolina is a no-kill shelter, so Rusty was welcome to live out the rest of his life there.

For the past three years, eight-year-old Kelli O'Rear had been volunteering at the shelter, helping to feed and groom the dogs. Her mother, Bobbi, is the shelter manager, and each day after school Kelli worked at the shelter caring for all the dogs.

Bobbi noticed that Kelli was taking a special liking to Rusty. "She would sit and talk to him, gently patting and brushing his coat, or sometimes pull out a stethoscope from her little 'doctor's bag' to listen to his heart. Some days, she would bring in a bag packed with brushes, toenail clippers, baby wipes, and perfume to pamper Rusty," recalled Bobbi. Kelli prepared Rusty's food (special gourmet meals) each day that she was there, and then in advance when she wasn't there so she knew Rusty was getting a nutritious diet.

One day, while Bobbi was cleaning out one of the dog's

cages, she turned to see Kelli kneeling at Rusty's pen with her head down, sobbing. "When I asked her what was wrong, I had to hold back the tears myself. She told me that she didn't want Rusty to die in the shelter without first having a home and a family that loved him," Bobbi explained. So it was decided that Rusty would finally have a place to call home. A place where he could live out his remaining years basking in the love of this caring little girl. Needless to say, Kelli was thrilled.

After six months in his new home, Rusty's once sad eyes now gleamed with happiness. Rusty's companion, Kelli, is a young spirit who is wise far beyond her eight years, and she is determined to make this world a better place for dogs like Rusty.

Kelli described her very best friend this way: "Rusty is such a wise old fellow. He reminds me of my grandfather who is gentle and kind to me. When I'm talking to Rusty and he is looking at me with his big brown eyes, I think I can see all the way down deep into his heart where he keeps all of his feelings and love. Sometimes he seems sad, but I think that's because he knows he'll never be young again, or maybe he's just tired. Spending time with Rusty makes me feel safe and happy, just like when I sit in my grandfather's lap. Old dogs like Rusty just want to be close to the people they love."

from UNFORGETTABLE MUTTS

Magic

TERRI CRISP AND SAMANTHA GLEN

Editor's Note: This story took place in Alviso, California, in 1983, following a major flood. The residents had been evacuated, and rescuers arrived to seek out animals in distress.

John and I had become friends. I admired him for his animal-handling abilities, and he respected my determination to learn. Together, we made a good team.

By the third day of the flood, the sky had lightened and the rain had weakened into a drizzle, interspersed with brief periods of the most welcome sunshine. We began our morning in search of a poodle named Fritz that had been left by his owner, locked in the bathroom.

"I figured he could climb on the back of the toilet if the water got too high," was the owner's explanation for leaving Fritz behind.

We were afraid he might be wrong.

The water had reached its crest, but it was receding slowly. As we headed in search of the poodle, we began to see new things along our way. Houses that we recognized only by the color or style of their roof were starting to have windows, porch lights, and doors. Mailboxes, fences, bushes, and swing sets were now protruding from the water. As we passed one house, John pointed to the wall that faced us.

"Look at the side of that place." I squinted in the direction John was pointing. My eyes were not accustomed to the sunshine that had just begun to peek through the clouds. I shaded my eyes with my hand to see better.

"Oh, yuck." Almost the entire side of the house was covered with snails.

"Not even floodwaters can kill them off," said John as we motored past. "I bet the cockroaches have all survived too."

I watched the snails until we turned the corner. In spite of not being particularly fond of them, I was amazed at how hard they had worked to stay alive. With agonizing slowness, the snails must have crept up the rough stucco surface, probably just millimeters ahead of the rising water.

By late afternoon we'd rescued twenty-seven animals, including Fritz. We'd found him shivering on the back of the toilet when we waded into the musty bathroom. The waterline had reached the bottom of the medicine cabinet. Fritz had definitely done some swimming.

We took all the animals we rescued back to our van, parked adjacent to the checkpoint, so our friends from the National Guard could keep an eye on them. When the van's cages were full, we'd call the Humane Society and they'd send a couple of kennel workers to transport the animals back to the shelter. Over the three-day period we'd rescued close to one hundred dogs and cats, and Pigsley, a three-hundred-pound hog.

Before we hauled our boat out of the water each afternoon, we'd make our evening feeding rounds. I was learning that in addition to having lots of stray dogs, Alviso had an abundance of cats too. Some of the felines were friendly but just too frightened to let us catch them. Most of them were wild. The cats had survived by climbing up on rooftops and clinging to tree limbs. We were their Red Cross, bringing food to these disaster victims.

We had just arrived at one of our feeding locations when a Coast Guard boat pulled up. We recognized the men on board. They had reported a stranded dog to us the day before.

"We've got another rescue for you. Apparently there are two Chihuahuas in a trailer behind the grocery store. You guys got time to get them?"

John looked up at the sky. I knew what he was thinking. We don't have much daylight left. "John, you go get the dogs. I'll stay here and feed this bunch."

"I don't know." John's concern about leaving me alone was evident.

"Oh, don't worry. I'll be fine. I promise I won't do anything *too* crazy." John had told me how important it is to work in teams when rescuing animals. This time he made an exception.

John helped me haul the bags of food onto the roof before he got back into our boat. "I'll be back before dark." That meant I'd see him again in less than forty-five minutes.

I didn't have to call the cats. The dinner bunch arrived from different directions, eager to eat. They circled and paced as I filled paper plates with mounds of dry food. Occasionally one would meow, as if to say, "Can you hurry it up?" Several of the braver cats got impatient and decided to eat right out of the bag.

In addition to feeding cats at this location, there were six plump chickens and an obnoxious rooster. I'd already scattered some chicken feed to satisfy them. They were busy pecking away as I laid down exactly thirteen paper plates. It was important to give each of the thirteen cats plenty of elbowroom.

With my job done, and not expecting John to return for a while, I sat down, stretched my legs out in front of me, and leaned back on my elbows to watch the feast.

This was the first time I'd stopped all day, and I suddenly realized how tired I was. It had been a long time since my morning coffee. A jump start of caffeine would sure have hit the spot. But caffeine wouldn't remedy the sore muscles.

Every part of my body ached, my arms the worst. In three days they had pulled me up onto roofs, lifted forty-pound bags of dog food, rowed our boat into places too full of debris to risk using the motor, cradled frightened animals, and carried a seventy-pound dalmatian two blocks through ankle-deep water because he didn't want to get his paws wet. Bandages covered the cuts on my forearm from my encounter with a cactus. Purple-and-green bruises were visible on bare skin not yet covered by bandages. I was basically a mess, but I was proud of my war wounds.

As the clouds overhead took on hues of pink and yellow, I got up slowly to refill some of the paper plates. A few of the cats had already finished and left without so much as a "meow" of thanks. A bulging black-and-white cat sniffed around her plate for any morsels that may have fallen off. She was the first to get seconds. I suspected her belly was full of kittens and not just food. I was scattering some more feed for the chickens when a familiar sound from the yard next door made me stop. Somewhere nearby there was a duck.

Now, granted we were in a flood, which if you're a duck must not be that unwelcome, but this duck sounded as if it was in trouble. I moved closer to the roof's edge, hoping to get a better look into the next yard. All I could see was water and floating patio furniture. Quietly I waited for the duck to make another sound so I could pinpoint its location.

Five minutes passed and the sound I'd been waiting for finally came. I moved to the north corner of the roof, and from there I could see to the far corner of the next yard. In a narrow space between a lopsided garage and a buckled fence was an enclosure roofed with chain-link fencing. Across its entrance was a makeshift gate, partially hidden by oleander bushes. The duck had to be in there.

I looked at my watch and estimated it'd be another fifteen minutes before John returned and I had just about that much good daylight left. Should I wait? Could I do this one on my own? I had promised John I wouldn't do anything too crazy! Another plea from the duck helped me make up my mind.

For a brief moment I hesitated. I felt like a kid again standing on the edge of my uncle Jim's swimming pool trying to get the courage to jump in, knowing how cold the water would be until I got used to it. I wasn't intending to go for a swim, but I knew the distance between me and the duck meant I'd have to get wet.

I sat on the edge of the roof dangling my legs over the edge. John had warned me the first day not to wear my waders into water deeper than my knees. Many a fisherman has learned the hard way—you fall in deep water with waders on and you may not reach the surface again. My waders lay crumpled in a heap on the roof.

It was hard to take the plunge. I turned around and lowered myself slowly into the murky water, trying not to think about the snake I'd seen slither past our boat earlier that day.

The water was colder than I had expected.

Holding on to the edge of the roof, I pulled myself through

the eight feet of water toward the fence that separated the two yards. When I got to the corner of the roof, I dog-paddled the short distance to the fence. Bushes buried below the surface tore at my jeans. I grabbed the water-logged wooden fence and held on.

"Okay. Over we go," I said to myself. My arms pleaded with me to reconsider. With both hands in place I pulled myself up until my stomach was teetering on the fence. I swung one leg over and sat straddling the wobbly planks. Feeling under the water with my sock-covered foot, I found the fence had a wooden brace that ran its length. It was just wide enough to balance myself on as I scooted along the fence in a sitting position. As I moved along the back fence, which leaned toward the yard behind it, I added a few splinters to my war wounds.

The roof on the back side of the garage hung over the fence. I now had to get off the fence and up onto the roof. The sooner I accomplished this the better, because the fence was becoming less stable. My rear end was first in the air as my hands grasped the fence and my one leg struggled to balance on the brace. At the most inappropriate moment a floating water bug decided to take refuge on my sleeve. He was in luck. I had no spare hands to shoo him away.

When I felt confident I wasn't going to go headfirst into the water, I raised the top half of my body ever so carefully. As I straightened up, my arms extended out from my sides for balance as I swayed to the right and then to the left, and the fence leaned even further. The water bug clung to my sweatshirt, hoping he wasn't about to go for a swim again. Dripping wet, I stood still.

Wasn't it about time for the cavalry to show up? I hoped to

hear the sound of John's boat approaching, but all I heard was the duck, reminding me he still needed help.

Pulling my left leg out of the water, I rested it on the top of the fence, while my right foot stayed planted on the brace. The image of a tightrope walker entered my mind. I may not have had a rope to balance on, but this fence was feeling just about as narrow. Bending forward, I reached for the corner of the roof. With a tight grasp on the wooden structure, I pulled myself toward my refuge. My left knee touched down on the shingled surface first. The right leg followed. With me safely on the roof, the fence finally gave way. Its timing couldn't have been better. The water had slowly eroded its supports, and the entire length of the back fence disappeared under the water.

Great! Now what do I do? I thought to myself. I'd have to figure out a new way back, but I didn't have time to think about that now. The duck's calls for help were getting louder and more insistent.

"Okay. Okay. I'm coming," I yelled to it.

Reaching the furthest corner of the roof, I bent down to peer over the edge. There he was. A large male mallard frantically swimming back and forth in the enclosed space below me. I now understood his predicament. He was trapped by the garage on one side, the fence on the other, the chain-link roof, and the closed gate. There was no escape from the pen.

I was surprised he was still alive. The space between the surface of the water and the man-made roof couldn't have been more than three inches high when the floodwaters had reached their crest. The duck must have continuously paddled as he struggled to keep his beak above water. There was now enough room for the mallard to swim, but this duck was ready to fly the coop.

It would have been nice if I could have opened the gate from up on the roof, but for some reason, nothing was to come easily for me that day. I realized I'd have to lower myself back into the water in order to free this duck, who by now was squawking nonstop.

A breeze was starting to stir, which reminded me how cold I was. I pulled my rain jacket tighter around my neck, but it couldn't prevent the shiver that started at my toes and moved to all parts of my soaked body. I rubbed my hands together, trying to warm them before I stepped down to balance on the side fence. Lowering myself into the water, I positioned myself at the entrance to the enclosure. I felt with my toes to see if I could reach the ground below me, but the water was still too deep. As I surveyed the situation the duck continued to voice his impatience.

With my left fingers hooked in the chain-link gate, I used my right hand to feel under the water for a latch. I dog-paddled to keep afloat. It didn't take long to locate the gate latch, which was not locked. Wiggling the metal rod, I freed the gate. Clinging to the gate with one hand and grabbing on to the frame of the garage door with the other, I very slowly pulled the gate out toward me. I was able to create a space just wide enough for the duck to squeeze through, and he wasted no time escaping. He paddled away and never looked back. Before he reached the end of the driveway, he spread his wings and took flight.

As he flew over the treetops, I hoped he'd always remain free.

I'd done it. I couldn't wait to tell John.

But then I realized my solo rescue was not yet over. I still had to get back to the roof where my waders and the bags of cat food were. I thought about staying put until John returned.

It would definitely be easier to get back up to that roof with his help, but I was beginning to get really cold. The risk of hypothermia entered my thoughts.

Just as I was beginning to plot my return route, I heard a noise from within the enclosure. *Please don't be a snake,* was my first thought.

Closing the gate wouldn't do any good. A snake could slip through the chain link with no problem. My only escape was to climb the fence.

Before I could raise myself to safety, I heard the noise again, but this time I realized a snake was unlikely to be the cause. It sounded like the thumping noise a rabbit makes with its back legs. Feeling somewhat braver, I peered into the enclosure. The noise came from the back end of the pen, which was about thirty feet long. My view was obstructed by pieces of scrap plywood leaning against the garage. I'd have to go into the pen to get a better look.

Clinging to the gate again, I managed to increase the opening so it was wide enough for me to squeeze through. My rain jacket got caught on a piece of metal and tore as I passed through it. With it came another scratch. Using the sagging chain-link ceiling to hold on to, I pulled myself along like a monkey hanging from a play yard jungle gym. Halfway into the pen, I discovered the source of the noise.

On a shelf near the back was the largest tan-and-white rabbit I'd ever seen. The water was within inches of covering the shelf that barely supported the animal. In the darkening shadows it was hard to see, but the rabbit looked as if he was okay.

"Hey, guy, what are you doing in here?" I couldn't believe someone had gone off and left yet another animal behind.

"I bet you'd like something to eat." John had packed some

rabbit food in the van that morning. "You cooperate, and I promise you dinner."

Slowly I moved toward the shelf. As I got closer I saw that the rabbit's fur was wet. He'd been in the water at some point. I hoped he wouldn't get scared and jump back in. Speaking softly to the trembling rabbit, I got closer and closer until I could reach out and touch him. He flinched slightly when he felt my hand against his back, but he didn't move. I worked my fingers up toward the area behind his ears and gently petted the damp fur for a few minutes.

"You ready to go with me?" I could see the rabbit's nose moving nonstop.

I was still in water too deep to touch bottom, so I had to use one hand to hang from the chain-link ceiling. With my free hand I pulled the rabbit toward me. His back feet kicked, but I used my arm to nestle him against my chest. I lowered my chin and quietly tried to reassure him. He calmed down.

I wasn't quite sure what to do next. I listened for the sound of John's boat again, but there was a lonely silence outside the pen. He must have run into some problems too, because he should have been back by now. It would be completely dark before too long. For the first time, I was scared. What if I got stuck in Alviso for the night? The thought of remaining in the floodwaters for much longer made me shudder.

"Okay, bunny, if we're going to get out of here, we'd better come up with a plan real fast. Any suggestions?" The bunny remained silent. "You're a big help."

Getting out of the pen was my first priority. With all the plywood leaning against the garage, I still wasn't sure that there might not be a snake sharing these close quarters with us. I decided to move out before one made its presence known.

Retracing my path was a lot more difficult with a hefty rabbit in tow. I had moved him up onto my shoulder, and using my chin, I tried to keep him wedged in place. I needed both hands to pull us out of the pen. It was slow going, and several times I had to stop and use one hand to reposition the rabbit. The gate was still wide enough for both of us to finally squeeze through.

Once on the outside of the pen, I had to figure out how to get both me and the rabbit back to the roof where my stuff was. With the rear fence down, it was like crossing a river without a bridge. My legs were starting to get numb, and a painful kink in my neck wasn't going away. I was running out of time. I'd have to swim to the fence that separated the two yards.

"Okay, rabbit, now you really have to cooperate. We're going for a swim."

I decided I'd try floating on my back with the rabbit on my chest, its body buried under my rain jacket. Whether this would work or not, I wasn't sure, but I didn't know what other choice I had. I slowly lay back in the water and struggled to stuff the rabbit under my jacket. Finally with his nose pressed up against my chin, we set off.

Our progress was slow, and several times I bumped into the patio furniture floating on the surface of the water. I remember staring up into the sky at one point and seeing the first star of the evening peeking out from the clouds. I'd not seen any stars in a week. The ever-present rain clouds had kept them well hidden. This seemed like a pretty good time to make a wish. "Oh, please, someone up there, work your magic and guide me out of this."

Just then I bumped into the fence separating the yards. We'd crossed our river.

My free hand grabbed the wooden plank, and I hung on. My teeth were chattering by now, and I was losing feeling in my legs. The rabbit wiggled under my jacket. "Hold on, guy, we're almost there."

There was one more obstacle in our way. I had to get both of us over the fence. I feared I didn't have enough strength left in my arms to pull us up. I was also concerned that I couldn't balance both of us if I made it onto the fence. The last thing I wanted to do was drop the rabbit. His chances of surviving would not have been good. And I'd worked too hard to save this bunny to have him drown now.

Just then, something bumped into my hip. A gurgling sound rose from under the surface of the water. I think I should have been scared, but for some reason I just remained still. Right in front of me, as I watched, a ladder slowly appeared from the depths of the floodwaters. It lay on the surface, within reach. Someone had worked some magic. We had our way over the fence.

Working quickly, with renewed energy, I positioned the ladder against the fence. With minimal effort I climbed the rungs, my rabbit still safely tucked under my rain jacket. I had just gotten us positioned on the fence, when a welcome sound penetrated the silence. It was John's boat.

"Well, bunny, we're safe, thanks to some very special magic. Magic . . . that's what I'll call you." I cuddled my new rabbit as we waited to be rescued.

from OUT OF HARM'S WAY

Trusting Babe

JANICE MARTIN

$\mathcal{B}$abe was a frightened six-week-old kitten when he came to live with us. He'd been the runt of the litter, a little on the thin side with skimpy black fur and big golden eyes.

I picked him up, and he immediately latched onto my hand with tiny claws and teeth. After prying Babe loose, I set him on the floor and filled a small bowl with milk. He sniffed it, then drank a little.

"Well, that's better," I said, and lightly stroked his back. He drew away from me, promptly disappearing behind the refrigerator.

I turned back to my sink full of dishes and hummed a lullaby I used to sing when our children were small. It was a singsong type melody meant to soothe.

I glanced over my shoulder as Babe slunk out of his hiding place and moved to the bowl. He watched me warily from the corner of his eye as he lapped up the milk. I wanted to tell him, "It's okay, Babe. I understand."

And I did. Coming from an abusive home, I, too, had to learn to trust. I started to speak, but then afraid he'd run off again, I just kept humming.

Over the next several weeks, Babe graduated from milk to dry kitty food and seemed to accept his place in our family, without really accepting us. He seemed to like having us around, especially when I hummed, but he hated being touched.

Babe grew steadily in direct proportion with the intake of his food and became a rather studly tomcat, marking his territory inside and outside the house. We remedied that situation with a trip to the veterinarian.

He was cranky when we brought him home, hissing at us and glaring with an accusatory stare. The only thing that seemed to calm him was my humming.

Months passed, and I waited for Babe to accept at least me—if no one else in the house—believing my love and patience would turn him around. But each time I tried to touch him, he'd cuff my hand with his sharp claws or run away. I'd start humming and remind myself, and him, that, "It's okay. I understand."

He refused to change and, finally, I accepted the fact that there was no room in Babe's heart for trust. Then I had abdominal surgery and came home to recuperate in bed with the help of family members and painkillers.

On that first day, I awoke to late afternoon shadows and a warm, furry hardness in the palm of my upturned hand. Babe lay stretched out full length along my side, his head nestled in my hand. I watched his rib cage lift and fall with his steady breathing. Impulsively, I drew my thumb across his forehead with a whispery touch. He opened his eyes, and I steeled myself for the pierce of his fangs.

Instead, he regarded me as casually as if he were checking out a bird too high in a tree to catch—annoyed but not interested in pursuing. Seemingly satisfied that I presented no real threat, he edged back and closed his eyes once more. We slept the day away. Except for intermittent sojourns on unsteady feet, the next three days passed this way, me on my back and Babe at my side, close, but seldom touching.

On the fourth day, I ventured out to my favorite overstuffed chair in the den, gingerly lifting my legs to place them on the footstool. Each movement elicited uncontrolled moans until I was completely settled. Babe had followed, hovering nearby, watching wide-eyed this once agreeable human being, now a quivering grouch, making her displeasure known without hesitation.

I expected him to scurry away. Instead, he did something that shocked me. He hummed. Not exactly a purr or a meow. It was a guttural hum, long and low, his head cocked to one side, his golden eyes scanning me from head to toe.

I laid my head in the crook of the chair wing and closed my eyes, then opened them to slits so I could watch him. Babe looked around as though not sure what to do next. I shifted slightly, which brought on another spasm of pain and more moans. Babe's chin snapped up and he began to hum again, a kind of singsong of purrs. Fascinated, I closed my eyes and listened, drifting to sleep. When I awoke, there was Babe hunched up next to my legs on the stool, but he wasn't touching or leaning against me.

He studied me for a moment, then stepped up on the arm of the chair and sought out my hand for a rub about his ears, his black fur soft and warm beneath my fingertips. Babe hummed his contentment, leaped to the floor, then sashayed away. His trust warmed me, and I started to hum my thanks, but a groaning pain gripped me once more.

Babe paused in mid-step and glanced back with a look that seemed to say, "It's okay. I understand."

Side By Side

SISSY BURGGRAF

I remember that night as if it were yesterday.

It was almost midnight when they arrived after their nearly twelve-hour journey. I recall walking around the trailer for the first look at my two new charges—two aged mares recently confiscated from their home by authorities.

They eyed me cautiously, non-trusting. We opened the trailer to unload them, careful not to allow more than a distance of six feet of separation between them because of the hysteria it would create. Standing outside of the trailer, it was as visible as the full moon above: the fear in their eyes that screamed, "How much more can we take? How long will this nightmare go on?"

We slowly led them down the aisle of the barn, past the curious eyes of their new stablemates, and once again, they were placed in a stall . . . together. They immediately rushed to a corner where they stood shaking, and with their heads merged in the corner. Only occasionally did the one, Dee, look around, and when she did, the fear in her eyes was undeniable.

We were overcome with concern for Rosie. Shaking and unable to lift her head, her eyes were hollow and distant; a dull blank stare where blazing light should have been. Lethargic, she refused to look at us.

I offered them small amounts of water and hay, but they ignored them. I monitored them through the night. Nothing changed.

It had been such a great day at the barn! Everything going right, the sun shining bright; everything perfect! Then I was shaken back to the reality of my job as owner of a horse rescue by answering a single phone call.

Ellen was an officer of a humane society located five hours from our facility. We had worked together on abuse cases before and I had learned "that" tone in her voice; a tone that meant something was terribly wrong. She asked if I had room to take two aged mares and continued to tell me the horrific experience she had encountered. I could only hope it wasn't as bad as she said.

According to Ellen, when the authorities arrived to investigate the horses, no hay, grain, or bedding could be found on the property. The two horses were literally eating the wood of the barn to try and stay alive. They had been kept, not only in the same barn, but in the same stall, for nearly twenty-eight years, being out of the barn only for transportation purposes.

We discussed the legalities of the situation, as we knew from the beginning that the owners would not cooperate with us, and if the health of the horses would permit them to make the trip. After deciding everything was a "go," Ellen said she would handle the procedures on her end and then call me. A few days later, she phoned. As expected, her dealings with the owners were a living nightmare. Several return trips to their farm and numerous phone calls later, they agreed to surrender the horses and a delivery date had been scheduled.

Now they had arrived and, to my sorrow, everything Ellen

had said was before my eyes. They were here, but tomorrow would be the beginning of my real challenge: to try to introduce these two terror-stricken horses into a life they had been denied for nearly twenty-eight years.

The next two weeks were spent just trying to gain their trust. My slow, deliberate movements stirred only more fear in the hearts where "fire and spirit" should have been held.

Tears filled my eyes when, a few mornings later, I entered the barn to find Rosie looking over her stall gate. When she saw me, her whinnies filled the barn. I approached her, talking softly, when I saw it! The very faintest hint of a spark in her eye! She and Dee still backed away and refused my touch, but it was another beginning.

I hung feed buckets in the stall, placing them so Dee and Rosie could touch one another as they ate, but they refused. They would eat only if allowed to share the same bucket. The same was true with water.

Five weeks had passed when I gained enough trust from them that I attempted to take them outside. This would prove more than I had imagined! Holding a lead line in each hand, I had to be sure they could feel one another before they were calm enough to handle. Their eyes once again filled with fear as they reluctantly followed me from the barn.

Neither had touched grass since the age of six months. Immediately they panicked! The whites around their eyes showing, nostrils flaring, they snorted and screamed as each of them tried to raise all four feet simultaneously. Terror showing in their eyes, I quickly worked to get them back in the barn and into their stall. There, they once again retreated into the corner where they shivered and shook with fear. I had lost everything I had gained . . . but only for a short time.

A week later I tried again. The experience was still trauma-
tizing, but they trusted enough to allow me to walk them a
short distance. This time, providing me fifteen minutes, I
would learn of their fear of birds, butterflies, water puddles,
and vehicles. But, this too, was a beginning. As of this day, it
would become a daily trek that would be lasting.

Soon, they trusted me enough that I could open their stall
door and they would run from the barn, make two laps around
the barn, and back to the stall they came! Always to the same
stall and always together. What a beautiful sight to see them
"trying" in a world that had been so cruel to them.

Two months would pass before I could separate them and
each would have their own stall. The stalls were side by side
with an open grid between them which enabled them to see,
as well as touch, each other.

I placed their hay bags back to back so it appeared they
were eating together. Each had her own hay, and plenty of it,
but they still feared the other would be hungry. Rosie would
take a bite of hay and eat it. The next bite would be dropped to
the floor where she would use her nose to push it under the
stall wall to Dee. Any hay that fell to the ground was "given"
to Dee.

Four months after the girls (as they had become known to
everyone at the farm) had arrived, I decided to try and turn
them out in a small paddock. Needless to say, this did not fare
well, either! They had seen only one other horse in their lives,
so when their stablemates began getting close to the fence that
bordered the fields, they once again panicked. The girls would
race one full lap of the paddock at top speed and then stand,
shaking, at the gate waiting for me to "save" them from their
newest danger. Every new step was an obstacle to them.

And it was always fun when the farrier came to do their feet! They had to stand in the aisleway together, touching, while he worked on them. This meant a lot of maneuvering to do all eight feet!

Thirteen months had now passed and it was time to try them with the other horses; time to see if they could lead a normal life. I turned them out in a small field with five other horses. The first few days Rosie and Dee stayed together in the run-in barn. Eventually, Rosie began to socialize and loved her new life. She would run and kick up her heels and "talk" to anyone who would listen. Dee, on the other hand, was reserved and feared her fieldmates. But, as always, Rosie and Dee were together at feeding time and Rosie always made certain Dee had enough to eat. At the end of the thirteenth month, Dee, too, began to live her life as a normal horse. She, too, began to socialize with the others.

The beginning of the fourteenth month would bring new changes for all involved with our horse rescue. For three years we had rented facilities and now we had purchased our own farm.

All of our horses, at that time numbering eighteen, loved the new land. Seventy acres of rolling hills to run and graze and enjoy life! Rosie and Dee would thrive on the lush pastures, with their nightmare past behind them. Finally! The light returned to Rosie's eyes and the fire and spirit to both their hearts.

I had once made the comment that when "the time" came, I hoped Rosie, the younger of the two, would pass away first. This time it was my fear that hung in the air. Fear of how Rosie would cope if something should happen to her beloved Dee. I had no idea how prophetic those words would become.

The world couldn't have been better, at least until the

Sunday morning I went to feed and Rosie didn't come to her bucket. This was unusual as she was always the first to her place.

I fed the other horses and then set out to look for Rosie. The search was short. Next to the fence, only fifty yards behind our house, lay Rosie. I called to her and she raised her head and knickered. She tried to get to her feet, but failed.

As I approached her, I called her name again, and once again she tried to stand. Again and again she tried, but her efforts were futile. Exhausted, she collapsed. Looking her over, I couldn't find anything wrong or see why she wasn't able to get up, but on closer inspection, I found it. It appeared to be a bullet hole between her eyes and was covered by her forelock.

I ran to phone the vet. After what seemed hours, he arrived. A careful examination determined what I feared: Rosie would have to be destroyed. I also phoned the sheriff; both, he and the vet, confirmed she had been shot with a high-powered rifle with a scope. A trespasser with a rifle outlawed in our state had once again shattered Dee's world and had stolen away Rosie's newfound life.

A reward was set and the search was now on for the killer of the beautiful white horse who, after twenty-eight years of abuse and neglect, had just learned to live. The sheriff advised us that Rosie was to be left in the field for at least four days. In the event the person was found, the bullet might have to be surgically removed from Rosie's brain as evidence to be matched with a specific rifle.

My concern now turned to Dee. Twenty-eight years she had lived, side by side, with Rosie. How would she survive now?

I covered Rosie with a heavy tarp and tied it, for her privacy as well as protection. When I returned the next day to feed, Rosie was uncovered and Dee was standing guard over her body. When I put grain in their buckets, Dee would paw Rosie's body and whinny to her. As I led Dee to her feed, she kept calling Rosie to "come to eat." When Dee finished eating, her guard duties continued.

For five days I would cover Rosie's body only to find her uncovered the next day with Dee by her side. The fifth day we would bury Rosie; but for nearly two weeks longer, Dee would continue to guard the place where Rosie had laid and continue to call her for supper each night.

It has now been two and a half years since Rosie's death. Her killer was never found although other horses within a ten-mile radius of our farm were also shot and had to be destroyed. Dee, at the age of 32 years, is now arthritic but otherwise in good health. She still lives her life in the rolling pastures of our farm.

Her trust has continued to grow. She comes to me when I call her and she can be handled as easily as a newborn kitten. The pain of her past seems to have faded away; but then, has it? I sometimes see that faraway look in her eyes and I can't help but wonder about what thoughts are passing through her mind. And as she stares across the vast fields, is she searching for Rosie? But I'm sure she realizes she'll never have far to go to find her. Rosie will always be with her, side by side.

WATCHING OUT FOR US

"Cast all your anxiety on him because he cares for you."

I PETER 5:7, NIV

When we love people, we care about their lives. We want to lift them up when they're feeling down. We listen to them when they need to talk, and when they don't want to talk, we just stay close to them. We touch their hand to let them know we're here. And, oh, when they're able to smile again, we join right in, and thank God for the joy!

We learned these things from our animal friends.

Ain't Nothing Better Than a Coonhound

JOAN EMBREE

$\mathcal{E}$ven though I loved Elvis Presley with each volatile hormone of my heart-wrenched fourteen-year-old self, I knew the way he denigrated hound dogs as he gyrated in his tuxedo on the Ed Sullivan Show wasn't right. There he was, on the small, round Magnavox screen that rested in its blond, wooden cabinet, crooning with pouted, swollen lips his near-grief that his hound dog was nothing because he never caught a rabbit. Thrusting his hips in distress, he called his dog a liar and said he was no kind of friend. The hound, wearing a top hat and perched high on a stool, looked mournful as Elvis ruthlessly tore his reputation to shreds. Even knowing Elvis was dead wrong about his dog, I admit that I too screamed with hysterical abandon, along with my four girlfriends who sat mesmerized each and every time he tossed his black, glistening hair and sexily sneered. Still, I wondered how that adorable hound made out in life.

I wasn't to meet a hound dog until I was a grown woman living in Washington, D.C. with my husband, Tim, and our two children, Isabelle and Blair, aged four and two. It was in the summer of 1972, when the city was held in a siege of unbearable heat and insect bliss. Locusts crooned their drone-chant day and night, their masses blackening the hazy sky, imbuing leaves and flower petals with big, gaping holes. Black brittle corpses of exoskeletons lay clustered like fallen armies at the base of trees. The city's humidity provoked a sub-army of slugs curled around the rims of teacups left out overnight on patios, their silver slime laying in wondrous, miniature trails.

Isabelle, Blair and I often sought refuge on the cool trails deep in Rockcreek Park. One muggy morning, as we strolled along singing Broadway show tunes, we heard a soft moan above our imperfect voices. We couldn't figure out where the sound was coming from. It was sad and intermittent, and seemed to emanate from several directions. We walked in circles trying to locate it, and finally came to a small mound at the edge of the dirt path, near a Magnolia tree. At first, we didn't know what we were looking at. Gradually, we recognized the mournful, blinking eyes of a dog. His body was raw-boned and meager, more bare than covered with fur. He was tied to the tree with a piece of ragged rope, left there to starve to death. What fur he had was clumped and matted with dried, black blood. Isabelle and Blair cried, "Oh, poor thing! Mommy, look at this sad dog!" I remember being struck by his beauty, his onyx jewel of a nose, the sable depth of his sooty-edged eyes, those long velveteen ears. Clearly, this was a hound dog, similar to Elvis's.

Our newfound dog didn't flinch as I scooped him up. He seemed light as a feather that had floated down from heaven and landed gently under a tree for us to find. We went immediately to the animal hospital where a doctor suggested it might be best to put the dog to sleep, considering how far gone the animal was. We wouldn't hear of that. It took only two months to nurse our coonhound back to health. This was not a difficult task. All he needed for a full recovery was lots of love, food and more love. We named him Sam, after Sammy Davis Junior, who could tap dance like no one else.

Not long afterwards, Tim was hired to publish a new magazine in Albany, New York, and so, we packed our bags, shipped our furniture, gathered up our four blue-gray cats and one fine hound and flew Allegheny (better known as Agony) Airlines into Albany Airport. Traveling with so many animals proved to be a harrowing journey. The cat carriers were placed on the revolving luggage belt, with gray paws sticking out of the airholes, scratching frantically in thin air. I felt horrified that some of the cats had almost escaped from the thick, but obviously not thick enough, cardboard carriers. The thought of them lost forever at the airport was appalling. A hideously, long pause ensued in which Sam's carrier did not roll onto the automated belt. When it finally did arrive, the children and I were so overcome with joy at the sight of Sam with his drooping ears, a pathetic and forlorn expression on his face behind the bars of the cage, that we laughed and hooted loudly. A woman standing nearby admonished us severely for what she took to be cruel glee at the sight of our dog's misery. She even threatened to report us to the humane society. But the more she scolded, the more we couldn't stop laughing. Tim, being reserved yet prone to droll humor, told the woman she ought to pity him because he suffered the great misfortune of sharing his bed with twenty-six feet other than his own.

We settled happily into a farmhouse nuzzled deep in gold, far-flung hayfields. The Housatonic River wound around lower meadows dotted with clover and purple thyme, from which rose two enormous, dark green haybarns. Blue, silver-misted

Berkshire hills undulated along the horizon like prehistoric beasts. Sam, howling and careening across the landscape, thought he had died and gone to heaven. On full moon, neon-white nights, he'd point his nose up to the sky, emitting soulful, unearthly howls, his long throat vibrating with ululations like a fine instrument. Even the coyotes would join in. To this day, I have not heard a symphony that could top the splendid and spine chilling ones of those nights.

Sometimes, when the wind knocks at my doors, scuttling dead leaves like crabs across an Autumn-stark lawn, moaning as it does behind the shutters, I imagine it also moves the ghost of Sam. It is then that I can see him, leaping over fallen logs in full pursuit of a lumbering woodchuck or a racing rabbit, his hound body lean and stretched as he ran into the darkened depth of trees. My memory's ear hears his howls, his "barking-ups," music destined to break your heart.

I am continually astounded at the presumption and igno-rance of people who say only human beings have thoughts and emotions, that the so-called lower forms of animal life function according to instinct. As if instinct itself isn't an ele-gant form of genius. Sam certainly dispelled this prejudiced notion. Indeed, he was a deep and profound thinker. You could see in his eyes all possible emotions: love, compassion, empa-thy, fear, sadness, happiness. Sam had great insight with the children and knew about the importance of sharing. For exam-ple, Isabelle would lick an ice cream cone, pass it on to Blair to lick, who in turn held it to Sam's salivating mouth. Sam did not, as one might expect, wolf it down. He'd take one polite lick, then turn his face to Isabelle, obviously saying, "Your turn, Belle."

Sam was good at problem solving, too. One afternoon, I was having lunch in our farmhouse with a new friend, thinking this was the civilized thing to do, when, in fact, I would have preferred being out in the fields with Sam and the children. Lunch began to feel everlasting and without end. I'm quite sure that Sam, my man, had decided enough was enough. He skulked unseen into the dining-room and slipped under the table, where he suddenly let forth a blood-curdling howl that caused both myself and my guest to drop our forks and simultaneously rise up from our seats. Having composed herself, the woman dared to peek under the table, whereupon she, in turn, let out a scream so deafening it sent Sam scrambling out from under the table to hightail it back outside. His long, velvety ears flew out like airplane wings and his eyes were wide with terror. I don't suppose he had anticipated so violent a reaction.

The woman stood, her hand delicately at her throat, and said, "Oh, dear, I'm afraid I have to be going. I feel rather ill." I looked under the table and there, neatly placed where her feet had been, was the severed head of a rabbit. The stem of its neck was scarlet and filleted to reveal ligaments, delicate and shiny like thin silver ribbons.

In addition to problem solving, I believe this episode showed that Sam was brilliant enough to understand that one thing can have many meanings. For example, had he laid the poor rabbit's head at my feet, it would have been recognized as a gift, as though he had bestowed me with a kiss. Sam knew I accepted him for who he was; an incorrigible hound with an insatiable need to hunt. Even though I didn't eat meat and I loved bunny rabbits, I didn't begrudge him his needs. I did try to scold him nicely, but it did no good.

And in return for my tolerance, Sam gave me more than I can say. He taught me how to see the beauty of the country, city girl that I was. Together we contemplated thin, winter moons slung like pale slices of eternity. We saw bird's nests made of moss and wool too perfect for art and too cunning for nature. We saw honeybees on white clover in fields of lean hay swaying in summer breezes, immovable plows in unmown fields, meadows dotted with swells of woodchuck homes, cows staring off into secret places beyond human vision. Sam, Isabelle, Blair and I slept among wild roses mangled into hedgerows, yellow yarrow, buttercups and cinquefoil splattered like abstract art.

One late afternoon, Isabelle and Blair, deciding to be independent and free, took off across the fields on their own. It was the first time I did not know their whereabouts. I raced through the house, calling for them. Then I tore across the fields and ran to the barns. They were nowhere in sight. I ran to the river, fearing the worst. Sam ran on ahead of me, weaving and circling, his nose close to the ground. Suddenly, he took off in the direction of a line of trees separating our property from that of our nearest neighbors, about two acres away. Although I tried to keep up with him, he left me far behind. Not long after, he returned holding the hem of Isabelle's negligee in his mouth, as he pulled her along. Her daily costume at that time was an old negligee of mine, red high-top sneakers and a rhinestone tiara. Blair ran behind them in his emerald green superman cape, the back of it emblazoned with a large, satin "S."

"Where did you two think you were going?" I scolded.

"We didn't think. We knew. We were going over to Harry's," Isabelle said in her usual forthright manner.

"He needed to see my cape," Blair said. Sam blinked at me. I think he was telling me to lighten up.

One late afternoon, a red pick-up truck pulled into our driveway, slowly, as if in a dream. The driver, a young man in overalls, walked stiffly over to where I stood in the garden, knee-high in Swiss chard. The children were on their swings, sailing high into the sky from the thick boughs of ancient maple trees, one tree growing next to the other. The man moved so slowly and bore no expression on his face.

He said, "You own a hound dog?"

"Yes, I do," I said.

"Afraid I have some bad news. You better come with me," he said kindly.

I got into his truck and we drove down to the main road. There was blood everywhere or so it seemed. Off to the side I saw Sam's limp body. Incoherently, I said, "Where's his head? I don't see his head. Maybe this is not my dog." I tried willing it to be the truth, that this could not be Sam. But I knew even before I saw Sam's face, that it was him. I knew by the colors of the crumpled body, the brick red-brown of his shoulder, the soft purple tones of the hollows of his belly, the chocolate-gray edge of his ear caressing the cruel road.

A deep, thick pain wrapped around my chest. It settled there for a very long time. I saw the blood in the road for weeks and months after rain, ice and snow had washed it clean. The winter became interminable. Tim rarely came home. I wanted to be happy again, to run in the fields and play with Blair and Isabelle, but my heart felt dragged down, like a stone or an empty clay vessel. I knew that somehow, if only for the children's sake, I had to wrench myself free of this grief.

Early one evening, I asked the children if they would run in the hay field with me, down to the river's edge. I asked if we could run as fast as possible, until our hearts pounded loudly in our ears. They thought this was a grand idea. We ran and ran, our mouths open and gasping. We tripped and rolled down on top of one another and wrestled on the cold, hard ground. I turned my face up to the blue-black, starlit night and called silently to God, asking him to rid me of my sadness.

A fierce wind came up out of nowhere. The night turned suddenly cold. I saw a shadow move out from behind a mulberry tree. A lean, shepherd-collie loped toward us. Even in the near darkness, I could see his golden coat, because he was surrounded by light. He had an air of confidence about him, as if he was not a stranger. He walked directly up to me and looked deeply into my eyes, gently taking hold of my wrist in his teeth, not hurting me in the slightest. He led me back down to the larger of the green barns. Isabelle and Blair followed along behind us. We climbed the haybale steps up into the barn and sat, the four of us in the wide, flung-open doorway, our faces turned to the river. We sat there quietly, obediently, hearing only the wind in the hills. The wind moaned, orchestrating black limbs of trees to rise up closer to heaven, moving ghosts along. Then we heard Sam. We heard his howls, the full range of them, mellow and mournful and full of music.

"Mommy," said Blair, "Sam is here again, only we can't see him."

"That's okay, Blair," Isabelle said, "at least we know he is home and happy."

"I think Sam told this other dog to move in with us," Blair said.

"Yes, of course he did. He's going to be our new guardian angel," Isabelle said in her usual doubtless manner.

We named our new dog Buford, after Buford Pusser, the sheriff in the movie, *Walking Tall,* who was brave and fearless like no one else.

from ANGELS WITH FUR

Mouse:
The Cat Who Cared

JOHN G. SUTTON

$\mathscr{P}$aul G. Stout had been a member of the U.S. Coast Guard for twenty-one years. He was a strong and active man, and his extensive duties, which included search and rescue missions at sea, made this a really exciting job. Then, after what seemed like a lifetime's service, he retired.

It was a shock at first. Paul missed the teamwork and the special sense of belonging that goes with it. But he was determined his working life would continue. So, after taking a further degree course in Phoenix, Arizona, he moved to the town of Kent about 20 miles south of Seattle in the state of Washington, where he had been promised a job. Living alone, he tried to make friends, but the locals seemed to have their lives to live and he was a stranger. It was a very lonely time for Paul and, when the job failed to materialize, he became deeply depressed.

Each morning Paul would rise early and walk through the fields and woods that surround the little town of Kent. There he could at least experience the beauty of nature and see the trees blowing in the soft wind coming in from the Pacific Ocean with salt on its breath. Back home, if his solitary apartment could be called that, he read the newspapers and applied for job after job. With growing anxiety, Paul realized that he had no one to turn to for help. Unlike most of the other folks in Kent, he was a man on his own and he worried that he would always be alone.

It was during the September of his first year in the new area that Paul discovered a litter of feral kittens. He had often seen the mother cat running wild in the streets near his apartment and had once fed her some fish bits left over from a meal. When the cat was about to give birth, she had found shelter under the wooden veranda outside Paul's apartment.

Quite what made him look there, Paul doesn't know. Perhaps it was the faint cry of the little kittens as they called out in hunger for a mother who could never return to feed them. For when Paul looked under the boards he could see the dead body of the wild cat, who had survived only a few days after giving birth. Gently he placed her lifeless body in an old box to bury later that day.

But now he had to do something for the living. He reached down and lifted the tiny kittens out from under the wooden boards. There were four of them, and all were desperately weak. Carrying them carefully in his hands, he took them into his apartment and placed them softly on an old towel. Their little eyes had barely opened and each tiny mouth was reaching for food. Rushing to the fridge, Paul found some milk and poured it into a saucer, but the kittens were too young to feed this way. Then he had an idea. In the bathroom he found an eyedropper. He filled it with milk and dripped the liquid into the kittens' mouths.

For hours and hours Paul cared for the kittens. They were brown and black, mainly, and very cute, but so tiny and weak. They seemed endlessly hungry and soon he was completely out of milk. Grabbing his overcoat, Paul ran out into the dark September night to buy some more from a nearby all-night store.

He couldn't have been gone more than half an hour, but when he returned, three of the little kittens were quiet and still. They were resting, Paul thought. But when he reached to touch them, their tiny bodies were already growing cold. In the short time it had taken him to fetch the milk, they had died. One by one he took each of the kittens outside and placed it in the old cardboard box next to their dead mother. For them life's struggle was over.

Back inside his apartment, Paul filled the glass eyedropper again and gently fed the surviving kitten. Right through the darkest hours he nursed it. The night turned into a pale dawn and still the kitten lived. "Come on, pal," said Paul to the little brown bundle of fur, no bigger than the palm of his hand. "You can make it if you try!"

There was something about this small creature that reminded him of someone. It had not a friend in the whole world, not even a mother to feed it or a sister to cuddle up to. This kitten was all alone. Then Paul realized—the kitten was just like him.

For a second his heart beat faster. They had each other now. Paul had the friend he had longed for all those months as a stranger in a strange town. Now, just as his life was slipping into hopeless despair, he had found another he could share each day with. No longer would he be alone. "Please God, let it live," he said and held the kitten close to his chest, as a mother might hold a newborn baby.

Over the next few weeks the kitten grew stronger. Paul fed it first from the eyedropper, then from his hand. To that kitten he was its mother and he cared for it with all his heart. The kitten was female and Paul called her Mouse, because she was little bigger than one and quite as cheeky. The little cat would jump up and sit on Paul's knee whenever she got the chance. Everywhere he went, there was Mouse, poking her funny face into the morning newspaper, into the cornflakes, into the sink; she was a proper nosy little cat.

Weeks turned to months and Paul had never been as happy. Mouse was his friend and each day seemed like fun with her around up to tricks. The cat followed Paul all over the place, getting stronger and stronger all the time. Until one day, just before Christmas, Mouse followed Paul out of the apartment on his early morning walk into the woods outside the town.

And from then on, each morning saw big Paul marching through the streets whistling a tune with a tiny tabby cat trotting along at his side. It might have looked odd, but it made Paul feel so proud. He had saved this cat, yet in a way the cat had saved him. Since he had taken little Mouse into his life, Paul had changed. No longer did he view each day with dread. Now he really had something to live for; now he had a friend that cared for him.

The new positive Paul quickly found a job. Perhaps there was something more likeable, more relaxed about him with Mouse as his pet. Somehow the love of that little cat had welcomed Paul into the community, made him feel truly at home.

Over the next eight years Paul shared every day with Mouse, the tiny pussycat. Everywhere he went she followed. Each morning, just as dawn broke, the two friends could be seen walking through the woods together, enjoying the fresh northwest wind blowing in from the sea. The salt breeze brought back happy memories to Paul's mind, of the days when his team consisted of more than a little cat.

Paul even bought another cat to keep Mouse company while he was at work. He called this one Briefcase, because one day the new kitten had trapped itself inside his case and caused quite a sensation when Paul had opened it at work. The two cats and Paul got on really well together, playing all sorts of crazy games.

Then, while still a young cat, Mouse became seriously ill. Paul did everything possible for his friend, took her to the vet and paid for the very best treatment, but nothing could be done. It was with a heavy heart that he made the final decision for his little Mouse. In all his years as a Coast Guardsman no decision had been harder to make.

That night Paul sat quietly in his apartment holding Briefcase on his knee, thinking of his friend. He remembered the day he had found the litter of kittens and how he had nursed the tiny Mouse. And he thought of all the joy her friendship had brought. Finding the kitten had helped him to find himself. To others Mouse might have seemed just a funny little cat, but to Paul she would always be the friend that came when his need was greatest. He knew he would never forget the cat that cared when no one else in the whole world did.

from ANIMALS MAKE YOU FEEL BETTER

Look Who's Teaching Whom

CHRISTIE CRAIG

When Ms. Higham walked into her classroom on the first day of school, and her first day at the Redd School, she took on sixteen first graders and . . . Sam. She had no problems with the children, this wasn't her first year to teach, but Sam, a floppy-eared rabbit who was expected to have free roam of the classroom, was another matter.

The first week went smoothly and teacher, students, and even Sam, found themselves in a good routine. However, as in most classrooms, a few behavior problems began to pop up. Ms. Higham who had always believed in discipline, was quick to set the rules. Certain behaviors led to time out and the child was not to return to his desk until he'd had an attitude adjustment.

Everyone understood the rules . . . everyone but Sam. For each time a child was placed in the designated spot, Sam would quickly hop over to the misbehaving child. Ms. Higham would always drop what she was doing, pick up Sam, look him in the eye and say, "Time out means time alone. Now be a good bunny and hop away."

But Sam was a persistent rabbit and refused to abide by the rules. On some occasions, even Sam got placed in time out.

Then one day, flustered by one very angry child, who had visited time out regularly, and tired of fighting a rabbit, Ms. Higham pretended not to notice Sam's quick trek to the time out corner.

From her desk, she watched as Sam nudged his nose against the little boy's ankle until he raised his head from his chest. She watched as the boy slowly began to stroke the rabbit and was amazed how the boy's angry expression softened, how his body language suddenly appeared less volatile. Shortly after, much quicker than ever before, the little boy rose from his spot and returned to his desk.

At first she thought it might be a coincidence, but the next few time out episodes proved her wrong. Time with Sam was much more effective than time out. And Ms. Higham who had always believed she could learn something from each and every student, was now being taught by Sam, a floppy-eared rabbit with a heart of gold.

A Distant Cry

KRISTIN VON KREISLER

One cool morning in Dobbins, California, David Giles was running the clothes dryer in his garage. When he stepped outside for a moment, away from the motor's hum, he heard an odd sound, like a bird call, yet unlike the sound of any bird he'd ever come across before.

Usually, he could identify all the birds in the Sierra Nevada mountains that surrounded his house. This call was a mystery. He shrugged, puzzled, and with his nearly deaf German shepherd, Ernie, started back toward his garage.

Before stepping inside, he glanced at the edge of the yard, where it dropped into a steep canyon. Staring intently down into it from the lawn was his cat, Bustopher Jones, a hefty black ruffian with a white "shirt front" and "spats."

Everything about the cat's expression and body language was saying, "There's something wrong down there," Giles thought uneasily. Bustopher was rigid and motionless. A frown wrinkled his forehead, his tail stuck straight out in a horizontal line, and he was pointing his right paw toward the trees below the yard. Pointing was a skill he'd recently acquired.

At the beginning of Giles's marriage to his wife, Marjorie, Bustopher had been an unseemly thug who shredded books, clawed his way up curtains, and used Giles's sofa for a scratching post and his Chinese carpet for a toilet. But moving into Marjorie's house had changed his behavior for the better. She'd sunk him into sheep dip to kill his fleas, and she let him roam outside to claw trees and dirt instead of furniture. Day by day, he'd become polite and considerate.

He had also picked up the odd habit of pointing like a bird dog. Whenever a deer wandered into the yard, the cat leaned back and aimed his right foot at the creature. Bustopher also pointed at birds, gophers, and moles.

Thinking perhaps that the cat had encountered some other animal, Giles crossed the lawn. When he was a few feet from the clothes-dryer noise, he heard the strange "bird" call again.

The closer Giles got to his cat, the more distinct the call sounded.

"Help me! Help me!" a woman cried faintly in the canyon. Her voice sounded at least a quarter of a mile away.

Giles left Bustopher, who still looked upset, and climbed with Ernie down into the canyon to investigate. As they traveled along a steep, circuitous route, Bustopher peered down at them.

"Help me!" the woman begged.

"I'm coming," Giles shouted.

"Thank God!" The woman started to cry.

As Giles got closer, he found Talma Crenshaw, age eighty-four, lying in a deep hole. She had gone down to turn off a faucet in her irrigation system and had fallen and broken her hip. For over an hour, she'd been lying on the cold ground in terrible pain and going in and out of consciousness.

Giles wrapped his jacket around her and ran to call an ambulance. He returned with paramedics.

"How did you ever hear me?" Crenshaw asked.

"I didn't. My cat did."

Looking down from the yard, Bustopher continued to oversee the rescue. He still appeared to be distressed about the stranger.

from THE COMPASSION OF ANIMALS

An Angel Named Max

CHARLENE S.

Eight months after my husband died, I accepted my cousin's invitation to take a job with his business in another city. Kent had always been a good friend, as well as family, and he argued that I should start over in a new environment that wouldn't be loaded with so many memories. He and his wife Eve would be happy to help us get settled.

My husband Joel had been a history teacher and the head football coach at the high school in the small Idaho community where we had lived for nearly ten years. At all the away games, Joel and the girls' physical ed teacher would drive a van with the cheerleaders while his assistant coach rode on the bus with the team.

On a foggy October night, the van had been struck at a railroad crossing by a fast-moving freight train. Joel, the physical ed teacher, and all but one of the five cheerleaders were killed outright. The girl survived, but would be confined to a wheelchair for the rest of her life.

After the funeral and a brief mourning period, a number of parents began preparations to sue the high school, claiming that Joel, who had been driving, had been at fault in the accident. Ugly rumors began to fly around the small town, even some suggesting that Joel, a firm, lifelong teetotaler, had been drinking.

Kent was right. It was becoming extremely unpleasant living in the beautiful village that we had loved so very much. Thankfully, he remembered my secretarial skills—and he claimed that he really needed a secretary now that his loyal gal Friday was retiring at the age of seventy-six. The timing was just right to relocate to the medium-sized city in Washington State where Kent had his factory. We moved in early August so that my sons, Shawn, eight, and Scott, six, could be settled before school started.

We had barely gotten moved into the small but attractive house that I had bought with the insurance money when the boys came home one day followed by a scruffy, mangy-looking cur. "Please, please, can we keep him?"

They had already named him Max, and there was no question that in spite of his woebegone, unkempt appearance, the mutt had a winning way about him.

And there was no question but that he was a stray, probably dumped on the streets by some irresponsible jerk who had grown tired of keeping him. He wore no collar, and he was skin and bones from lack of proper nourishment. I'm no expert, but I guessed that with his medium-length, yellowish hair, he was some kind of Labrador-setter mix.

If we were to keep him, I told the boys, we would have to have a veterinarian check him out. Shawn and Scott cheered in unison, interpreting my warning as consent.

The vet, a seemingly cheery man in all other respects, was not at all positive about our keeping Max. After a rather extensive examination, he guess-timated Max's age at around two years; then he rattled off at least half a dozen ailments that he suspected Max harbored, and he listed several more shots and pills that Max should have immediately. In answer to my legitimate query as to how much this would cost me, he shrugged and rounded off a fee at around seven hundred dollars.

My knees buckled. After the move, the purchase of the house, and buying some new clothes suitable for work, I was nearly broke. Seven hundred dollars would just about clean out the cupboard until my first paycheck.

"Mrs. S., my advice, if you want it," he began—then taking notice of Shawn and Scott for the first time, dropping his voice to a whisper—"is to let me put the dog to sleep. I don't think he's worth saving. And he's certainly not worth that much money."

He had not lowered his voice nearly enough. Shawn understood the euphemism of putting a dog "to sleep," and he quickly translated for Scott. Tears brimmed in their eyes.

"No, please, Momma," Scott pleaded. "Let him live, please."

My sons had had too much of death in their young lives. I told the vet to begin patching up our dog so we could take him home with us as soon as possible.

Even Kent was critical of my decision, arguing that if I wanted to get the boys a dog, he had a friend who would sell us a purebred at a very reasonable price, less than I would be paying in veterinarian's bills for a mutt of absolutely no pedigree whatsoever. I asked him to be understanding. As far as Shawn and Scott were concerned, it had to be Max.

By Christmastime, we had had Max for four months. He had regained his health—and his appetite. He had filled out into quite a handsome canine, and he seemed to bring some kind of balance to Shawn and Scott that had made their adjustment to new schools and a new community much easier.

Because of the meaning that he brought to my sons' lives, I overlooked the bills that demonstrated that he was nearly eating us out of house and home. And he wasn't satisfied with crummy old dog food and scraps. He had developed a sweet tooth and would sit up and beg for chocolate chip cookies.

Even worse than his bottomless tummy was the fact that Max seemed never to stop shedding hair. His yellowish strands would stick to the sofa, drift across the carpet, end up in the laundry, and even float up to our plates at mealtime.

But in spite of all these minor irritations, I had to admit that I loved Max as much as the boys did.

Three nights before Christmas, Max awakened me by pawing at my covers and whining. I had been working overtime at the office to get extra holiday money, and I did not appreciate his intrusion into my room.

"Just let me sleep and get out of here, you bad dog!" I scolded him. "You know my bedroom is off limits when I'm sleeping! Bad dog!"

His response was a sharp bark that hurt my eardrums.

And then I sat up, wide awake. Max always slept between the boys. In four months he had never entered my bedroom at night.

Something was wrong.

Then I noticed that the power on my alarm clock wasn't working.

Figuring that we had experienced a power outage, I slid my feet over the side of the bed and into my slippers. I had foolishly left on too many Christmas lights and had blown a fuse, no doubt. Max had probably become upset by the sudden darkness in the house.

As I stumbled around my bedroom in the dark, Max kept barking that shrill, ear-piercing yelp.

Would he be that upset by the darkness? Or was something else wrong in the house?

When I opened the hall closet where the circuit breakers were located, I nearly fell to my knees in horror. There was a huge wall of flame and smoke inside. And my opening the door had caused smoke to billow out in dark, suffocating clouds. I began to choke in uncontrollable spasms as I staggered backwards.

The fire had obviously burned out the circuit breakers so the smoke detectors couldn't go off. The flames and the smoke had been traveling up the inside wall of the hallway, eating away at the house's very structure.

I was trembling in terror. Would I even be able to get to the boys' room before the walls and ceilings were engulfed in flames? The smoke moved around me in smothering clouds that made me choke and gasp and blinded my vision.

Just as I was about to panic, Max took my wrist in his mouth and led me through the smoke to the door to my sons' room.

I hesitated, afraid to open the door. What if their room, too, was filled with flames? What if Shawn and Scott were already burned alive?

I thought I would collapse with fear. If the boys were dead, there was no reason for me to live. I would just lie down and give up and let the flames take me.

Max shook my wrist, as if prompting me to stay focused, to stay centered. I opened the door and saw to my relief and joy that it had only just begun to fill with smoke.

Once inside the room, Max barked sharply, then bounded to the double bed to nudge Shawn and Scott into wakefulness. Although they were understandably dazed and confused, Max shepherded them toward me, then led us all through the thick smoke to safety out the front door.

Although the fire department arrived within minutes, our

house sustained heavy damage, forcing us to accept lodging with Kent and Eve until we could find a new home.

"Max saved our lives, didn't he, Momma?" Scott asked as I was tucking him and Shawn into bed in their guest room.

When Shawn and I readily agreed that Max was a hero, Scott corrected us by saying that he was an angel.

"After Daddy died," he told us, "I prayed that God would send an angel to watch over us. I knew he heard me when he sent Max to protect us. Now Max even worked a miracle and saved us from a burning house. He is a real angel for sure."

from ANIMAL MIRACLES

The First Cat

RENIE SZILAK BURGHARDT

When my nineteen-year-old mother died two weeks after giving birth to me, I inherited her cat, Paprika. He was a gentle giant, with deep orange stripes and yellow eyes that gazed at me tolerantly, as I dragged him around wherever I went.

Paprika was ten years old when I came into this world. He had been held and loved by my mother for ten years of his life, while I had never known her. I considered him my link to her. Each time I hugged him tightly to my chest, I was warmed by the knowledge that she had done so too.

"Did you love her a lot?" I would often ask Paprika, as we snuggled on my bed.

"Meow!" he would answer, rubbing my chin with his pink nose.

"Do you miss her?"

"Meow!"

"I miss her too, even though I didn't know her. But Grandma says she is in heaven, and is watching over us from there. I think it makes her happy that we have each other." I would always say, for it was a most comforting thought to my childish mind.

"Meow!" Paprika would respond, climbing on my chest

and purring contentedly. I was convinced he understood me, and I knew I understood him.

At that time we lived in the country of my birth, Hungary, and I was being raised by my maternal grandparents because World War II had taken my young father away. As I grew, the war intensified, and soon we were forced to become migrants in search of safer surroundings.

In the spring of 1944, when I was seven, as we traveled in a wooden wagon pulled by 2 horses, Paprika and I snuggled in the back of the wagon. During the numerous air raids of those times, when we had to scramble to find safety in a cellar, closet, or ditch, he was always in my arms, for I refused to go without him. How could I, when one of the first stories I was ever told as a child was that of my dying mother begging her parents to take care of her baby as well as her cat?

During the Soviet occupation of our country in the early spring of 1945, as we emerged from a bunker where we had spent a terror-filled night, Paprika made friends with a young Russian soldier, who treated him to tins of sardines, because he reminded him of his own cat back in Russia! And always, during the trying times that persisted in our country, Paprika's love made things easier to bear for me.

By the fall of 1945, Grandfather had gone into hiding, to avoid being imprisoned as a dissident by the new communist government. The solemn Christmas Grandmother and I expected turned into my worst nightmare when I awoke on Christmas morning to find Paprika, still curled up next to me, lifeless and cold. He was nineteen years old, while, I, only nine, vowed never to give my heart to another cat.

Christmas 1951 was our first Christmas in our wonderful new country, the United States of America. The horrors of war, the four years of hardship in a refugee camp were behind us now, and a new life filled with hope lay ahead.

On that Christmas morning, I awoke to a tantalizing aroma wafting throughout the house. Grandmother was cooking her first American turkey. And one of the presents under the Christmas tree seemed alive, for it was hopping around to the tune of "Jingle Bells" playing on the radio. I rushed over, pulled off the orange bow, and took the lid off the box.

"Meow," cried the present, jumping straight into my lap and purring. It was a tiny, orange tabby kitten, and when I looked into its yellow eyes, the old vow I had made in 1945 crumbled away, and love filled my heart once again. And there have been many other cats over the years. But the memory of the first cat shall remain close to my heart as long as I live.

Honey Hurricane

MERRILY WEISBORD AND KIM KACHANOFF, D.V.M.

The sun shines brightly on two-year-old Honey Hurricane as she takes her last run with Jean near the pond behind their prison housing unit. Jean has known this day would come ever since she was first given Honey to train as a service dog. Honey, a cross between a cocker spaniel and a Nova Scotia duck tolling retriever, has been her inseparable companion for almost a year. And Jean has loved her and bonded with her as she has with no other creature

Today it is time to say good-bye.

They walk slowly to the canine room in the main building of Nova Institution, a medium-security prison in Truro, Nova Scotia. The room is filled with fluorescent-lit plants and images of women and dogs, including the participants of the Pawsitive Directions Canine Program. Jean Reynolds, a tall thirty-eight-year-old with a shock of curly brown hair, crouches down to be close to tiny, golden-brown Honey Hurricane, who stands less than knee high.

No long good-byes. Jean wraps her arms around Honey and gives her a final kiss. Honey seems subdued. She doesn't leap up on Jean or show excitement. "After all the time we spent together, she knows something is going on," Jean quickly realizes. "She's probably been picking up vibes from me all week."

Jean strides toward the door to return to her room. Normally, Honey would accompany her. But, today, when she faithfully follows, Jean turns and says, "You stay here, Honey."

Honey's round brown eyes soulfully follow Jean's retreating figure. She curls up in a tight ball on the floor, waiting out this latest change in a young life filled with turbulence and transformation.

Honey's known biography begins in the Colchester County pound. Animal control officer John Sitser found her starving and abandoned, running wild on the streets of Truro.

She was pacing in an outdoor pen with five or six other yelping dogs when Heather Logan came to adopt a dog for the prison canine program. According to pound rules, Honey would be destroyed if nobody adopted her within the next forty-eight hours.

Heather, a no-nonsense dog breeder and trainer with thirty years' experience, checked out the dogs. Her adoption guidelines were strict: no dogs with even the slightest sign of aggression; and no guard breeds such as German shepherds, who could potentially be trained to protect the prisoners against the guards.

"Are you interested in this little brown dog?" asked animal control officer John Sitser.

Based on her breeding, Honey had the credentials to fit Heather's bill. Cocker spaniels are highly intelligent, friendly, and exuberant. As an added bonus, they are often hopeless guard dogs. Jaunty, animated Nova Scotia duck tolling retrievers—tollers, for short—were developed in the nineteenth century to attract and retrieve ducks. The flash and bounce of the white points on their paws, chests, and tails seemed to lure ducks to the blind. Tollers are smart, devoted to children and families, and take well to obedience training. Like cocker spaniels, they can be wonderfully inadequate guard dogs.

"No," Heather answered inexplicably, and she left, alone.

Ten days later, Heather came back. And, surprisingly, Honey was still there. Once again, softhearted John asked Heather if she wanted the little brown dog. Once again, Heather said no.

Another ten days passed, and when Heather returned to the pound, Honey was still there. John saw something special in her and thought she'd make a really nice pet. That's why he hung on to her. This time, John insisted on knowing why Heather wouldn't take her.

Honey jumped at the wire fence, trying desperately to capture Heather's attention. Heather considered John's question and realized that her refusal was based completely on personal prejudice. "Spaniel-like dogs don't seem to get along with me," she admitted. "They've bitten me many times in the past thirty years."

In order to be fair, Heather agreed to behavior-test Honey, to see if she allowed herself to be handled and to ensure she was not aggressive.

John opened the cage, and Honey bounded out, wiggling and wagging her tail, straight into Heather's arms.

Meanwhile, at Nova Institution, inmate Jean Reynolds successfully completed phase one of the three-phase canine program, covering the theory of canine behavior and training. She then asked Heather hopefully if she could have her own dog to train, a large, black male, if possible.

When Heather returned to Nova, she called Jean to meet her out front.

Jean saw her approaching in the distance, with a little brown creature flipping around at the end of a leash like a hooked fish.

"Here's your dog," Heather said, "except she's not large, not black, and not male."

Jean looked at the dog. The dog looked up at her and it was love at first sight. Jean got down on her knees, and although Honey was filthy, she enveloped the small dog in a tight hug.

"Oh, honey," she sighed. Then she thought a moment and smiled up at Heather. "That's her name."

A few days later, with a better understanding of her new dog, Jean added the surname Hurricane. Honey Hurricane was everywhere at once, getting into it all.

Jean and Honey began training, two newcomers on a journey together. Jean's experience with animals was limited and Honey, the street survivor, growled defensively whenever other dogs approached. She launched herself ferociously at Heather's massive German shepherd. Jean was horrified, thinking that Honey was about to become lunch, but the larger, gentle pet was well-behaved.

Honey's socialization began with a down-stay command and a gradual acclimatization to being circled and stepped over by eight other dogs. As long as she stayed down, Jean praised her lavishly and handed out goodies, until Honey understood that staying down earned her treats. Eventually, she learned to remain still for longer and longer stretches.

Next was heeling. Jean placed a strip of tape on the side of her left leg, just below the knee, as a marker. Honey had to control her exuberance and stay within six inches of the little piece of tape. Heeling calmly by her trainer didn't come naturally. "We played statue a lot," Jean recalls. Whenever her dog rushed ahead, Jean stood still until Honey caught on that she wouldn't get anywhere faster by racing ahead.

At the end of November, three months after Honey and Jean met, their relationship was abruptly terminated by Jean's parole. Thrilled to be out of prison, Jean bade Nova adieu, and wrote a heart-wrenching farewell poem to Honey.

> *Even when we're far apart*
> *I'll hold your memory in my heart*
> *The bond we share no one can break*
> *Though when you're gone my heart will ache.*
> *So here's my heart*
> *It belongs to you*
> *I love you, Honey,*
> *You know I do.*

Honey returns to the kennel at Heather's to await a new trainer. Jean heads to Halifax, violates her parole conditions by drinking, and within three weeks is returned to Nova with no guarantee of getting Honey back. And now she needs and wants her more than ever.

Then Jean gets good news. She is being given another chance in the canine program. Honey rushes up to her, tail wagging, ecstatic to see her again. After weeks of being just "a happy kennel dog," Honey's skills have regressed, but she is blessed with high intelligence and a persistent nature. The team quickly falls into step with each other, deepening their bond and undertaking more advanced training.

Most mornings, the other three dogs sharing their house leave their trainers' rooms and galumph into Jean's room for a doggie rumpus. Then Honey and Jean take a long walk around the grounds, often with at least one other inmate-dog team. While Jean works in maintenance and horticulture, Honey returns to her crate in their room. For at least two hours every weekday, rain or shine, Honey and her mistress walk together. They also spend an hour training with Heather, practicing everything from skipping rope in tandem to retrieving a soft drink from the fridge. Weekends, Jean and Honey often spend five hours together walking, training, and enjoying each other's company.

In April, after eight months of training, Jean learns Honey is going to the Braeside Nursing Home to start her career as a nursing-home assistance dog. To further prepare her for her new job, Jean teaches Honey to lay her head quietly on her knee and wait to be petted. She plays "old lady" with a walker, making sure Honey stays clean of her uncertain movements. Using a wheelchair, she helps Honey readjust her previous heeling technique. Honey learns to let the wheelchair move through the door first before returning to a proper heel. Finally, Jean introduces a bell hanging by the door, so Honey can ring it to attract attention when she needs to go out.

At the end of the month, Honey takes her Canine Good Citizen test, administered by the American Kennel Club. She demonstrates her proficiency in the fundamentals of dog obedience, including greeting new dogs, heeling, and walking on a loose leash. Eight months earlier, Honey had instinctively attacked a large German shepherd. Now, having passed her tests with flying colors, she is officially decreed a model canine citizen.

Soon after, Jean is released from prison.

Three days later, Honey moves to her new residence,

the Braeside Nursing Home in the tiny village of Middle Musquodoboit.

Honey lies awake in her spacious metal crate in the activity-planning office at Braeside Nursing Home, on the banks of a peaceful river valley. She is partly covered with a pink blanket, her rope toy and bone beside her. It's 6:30 A.M., the time she used to awaken beside Jean, leaping all over her bed, covering her with kisses, begging to run outdoors right away.

A staff member unlatches Honey's crate and wishes her a cheery good morning. Without further ado, the new nursing-home assistance dog bounds out, eager to start the day.

Her white paws pad down the pastel-painted hallway, through the activity room, and straight to the back door. Honey makes a beeline for the fenced-in yard and, true to her retriever self, tears around enthusiastically until she's spent. She rests briefly in the shade, tracking the birds overhead until it's time for morning rounds.

Cathie Risser, the personal care worker primarily responsible for Honey, sets the room-to-room pace. Honey seems to know instinctively how to behave with those in wheelchairs and those with dementia or Alzheimer's. She approaches them slowly and moves gently near them.

Esther, who has severe dementia, speaks rarely, and when she does, it's one labored word at a time. Cathie positions Honey in front of the elderly resident and the old woman's hands immediately seek out her soft fur.

"You're some cute dog!" Esther says effortlessly.

Cathie rewards the friendly dog with a handful of dried food. Honey was trained using a method called operant conditioning. Based on the principles of psychologist B. F. Skinner, operant conditioning uses only positive reinforcement, and Honey's daily ration of dog food is meted out one treat at a time all day long. She earns her tasty reinforcement by working, embedding the notion that positive behavior leads to concrete rewards. Cathie wears a pouch with treats on her waist and a bowl of food sits on the counter near the door for other staff members to use.

The four white paws continue along to Alice Cook's private room. It's the first of Honey's thrice daily visits. Alice is already seated near the window when Cathie arrives. Her face lights up when she sees Honey. Should Cathie ever visit without her four-legged assistant, Alice's first question is, "Where's the dog?" She opens her arms and Honey leaps up on her lap and lays her head on Alice's shoulder in a gracious canine hug. Alice knows how her visitor loves to be petted, and with trembling hands she strokes her long fur, dog and human almost purring. For Alice, it was hard to leave her dairy farm and her big old house to come to Braeside nine months ago. But the hardest part was leaving behind her collie, Keesha. Widowed for twelve years, Alice had treasured Keesha's companionship. Now, when Cathie waves good-bye, she leaves a new canine friend with the resident. Honey remains, always nearby but never underfoot, keeping Alice company.

Honey visits from room to room, cheering the residents with her warm, life-affirming presence. When she's invited, she jumps up onto the bed, laying her head on a resident's lap, waiting to be petted. When she first arrived, she was so excited about her new surroundings, she couldn't sit still for a moment. Now she can lie quietly for short periods, while gentle hands stroke her head. Cathie encourages her with treats, hoping that eventually Honey will settle in for prolonged periods, offering comfort to those who are frail and bedridden.

At 8:00 A.M., Honey returns to her pink blanket for a much-needed break. While the residents eat, she rests, preparing for more morning visits. As with any nursing-home worker, there's a danger of burnout. Being constantly enthusiastic and energetic with so many people can be exhausting. Honey stretches out and enjoys the downtime.

By mid-morning, she has visited everybody who wants her company, and she's ready for another run outside. A cowbell hangs waist-high at the back door for Honey, but for some reason she doesn't like its sound. She jumps up next to it, but avoids ringing it. When a staff member goes out to grab a breath of air, she dashes out, darting left and right, scampering around the picnic table, churning up the yard with her little legs.

A decorated pineapple sits on the table in the small kitchen area; a mechanical parrot flies in circles from a center ceiling beam; and the Hawaiian luau begins. Honey dashes around the activity room, trailing a tissue-paper lei from her mouth, twisting her head back and forth, toying with the lei until it shreds. She spots the mechanical bird and her hunting-dog instinct awakens. She jumps at it with youthful abandon.

Cathie hands out Hula Hoops to two volunteers and calls Honey to participate in a little entertainment. The volunteers hold up the hoops in a row. Honey sits. Then Cathie commands, "Hoop, hoop, bell!" and Honey vaults through the hoops, heading for her target—the cowbell at the door. She leaps toward it, veers to the side in mid-jump, and bypasses the bell, nosing the doorframe instead.

"She faked me out!" Cathie whoops, remembering Honey's aversion to the sound of that bell.

Honey drifts out of the room and sees Hugh, dressed in a red shirt and blue slacks, sitting in his wheelchair. Nobody knows what's on Hugh's mind, since he rarely speaks, and when he does he is not always lucid. Honey visits him at least three times a day.

"Where's your puppy?" Cathie asks him, as she moves to the side of his wheelchair and taps his knee.

"Knee," she says to Honey.

Honey places her head on Hugh's knee and waits there patiently. Cathie reaches into her pouch to hand Hugh the doggie treat, and his eyes shine merrily as his fingers close around it. He hesitates slightly, then offers it to her, remembering from her many visits how gentle she is.

Cathie redirects Honey's attention to Martha, fidgeting nervously on the couch beside Hugh's wheelchair.

"Get out! Get out!" Martha yells, lifting her cane.

"You liked her this morning," Cathie reminds her. "You were calling her kitty-kitty!"

"I don't want a bit of it," Martha responds, but a smile creeps across her face. Cathie takes the old woman's cane-free hand and gently places it on Honey's back. Martha begins caressing Honey, slowly, rhythmically. The small brown dog snuggles in close. As she repetitively strokes the soft warm fur, Martha's blood pressure stabilizes. By the time the luau is over, she is fast asleep.

In the early evening, Honey does her final rounds, including another trip to Alice's room. Alice invites her onto the bed and takes out her dog brush. Honey flips over on her back, legs stretched in the air, waiting to be petted. Then she rights herself, tail wagging in anticipation as Alice's trembling hands lift the brush and lovingly run it down the length of the little dog's back. As Alice strokes, her shaking completely ceases and her movements become firm and calm.

At the community college in Truro, where she's studying to become a veterinary assistant, Jean still thinks of Honey and the bond they shared. "Honey needed a whole lot of love, and I had a whole lot to give her." Jean realizes that, through her dog, she experienced a unique love that gave her confidence and changed her life profoundly.

Now, Honey takes all the love Jean first gave her and shares it with a dozen elderly people. As Alice fondly untangles the feathery knots behind the little brown dog's ears, she sighs contentedly. "With Honey here, this place feels more like home." Once again, Alice has someone loving to care for.

Nightfall ends Honey's long shift. She eats a last evening snack and curls up in her cozy crate, a small castaway mutt graced with the gift of reawakening love and hope in all those her little body touches.

from DOGS WITH JOBS

Ode to Bob Dog

BRENDA RANDOLPH

My dad's name is Bob, so I guess it was only fitting that his dog's name was "Bob Dog." I don't remember exactly how Bob Dog came to my dad but it was about 15 years ago when Dad got Bob Dog as a pup. Dad needed a good cattle dog and since Bob Dog was a mix of blue heeler and border collie, he fit the bill perfectly. Bob Dog learned quickly and soon became a one-man dog. He seemed to understand a very wide variety of directions only if they were given by my dad.

Living in a small Ozark community where everyone knows everyone and their dog, plus all the lineage of both, it wasn't long before Bob Dog earned his reputation as a good "cow dog." They also knew he was very temperamental and protective of Dad's truck. Most people quickly learned this fact one way or the other, sooner or later.

Bob Dog had his own house in the back of the farm truck and when Dad told him to "stay," he stayed! Many times Bob Dog looked friendly enough, but when someone crossed the invisible line over the truck bed, he was known to turn quickly and take a bite out of that person's arm.

We all worried about the liability of Bob Dog. We repeatedly warned Dad, "You are going to get sued one of these days!" The older Bob Dog got, the less we learned to trust him;

that is, all but Dad. Bob Dog even bit my small nephew one day when Patrick accidentally got too close to the truck. Fortunately the wound was not severe enough to scar. Surely Dad would do something with Bob Dog now. But, no, he loved his dog and his dog loved him, so he continued to make excuses for him while the rest of us just shook our heads.

Not only could Bob Dog save many a step in the pasture, he was known far and wide for his ability to track a wounded deer during deer season. Many a time a hunter would come to the house to ask to borrow Bob Dog. My dad would simply take him out to the woods and say, "Go find it," and he would! Dad was always so proud and gloated immensely about how truly smart Bob Dog was. Then he'd laugh and say, "You'd better not get too close to him now. He's a little cantankerous."

Bob Dog's true worth became known several years ago when my dad rode his ATV out to check on the calving cows. Dad found an old cow down and having trouble with the birthing process. As he was bent down pulling the cow, the cow jumped up and kicked him so suddenly that he didn't have time to get out of the way. She was charging at him again when Bob Dog flashed in between the cow and my dad. He held the cow at bay until my dad could collect himself. Losing his glasses, my dad had to grope along the ground until he found a large tree to crawl behind. As Bob Dog continued to bark and circle the cow, Dad rested, checked his injuries and contemplated his next move. He was then able to mount the ATV and slowly ride home with Bob Dog protecting him all the way.

When Dad made it to the house, he was in bad shape. After getting him to the hospital, we found out he had a broken nose, several ruptured discs in his back and cuts and scrapes everywhere. Though the bond between man and dog had been tight, it was irreversible now. Dad still swears Bob Dog saved his life that day. The cow attack certainly had lasting effects on Dad's mobility, but he and Bob Dog soon were back doing the things they loved.

Bob Dog continued to protect my dad, even when he too was arthritic and old. But after many years, it was Dad's turn to take care of Bob Dog by helping him in and out of the truck.

With his last bit of energy, Bob Dog would even help train several of his offspring. When they beat him to the cow, Bob Dog seemed to know it was time to go to the truck. He would retreat to his bed in the back of the truck for a little rest.

Too feeble to go too much, Bob Dog was now about thirteen. His home was a blanket in the garage, a donut for breakfast and Oreos for snacks. Still, these special treats were to be fed to him only by his master.

Mom never liked Bob Dog much for fear of him, and she was liking him much less now that he had decided to take up residence in the garage. Dad never acknowledged Mom's fear or dislike of the mess. Bob Dog would lie wherever Bob Dog wanted to lie.

My dad became very ill last winter with pneumonia. As mother was preparing him for the trip to the hospital, Bob Dog sensed that things were not well with Dad. As my mom was helping Dad out the door to the car, Bob Dog nuzzled Dad and whined as if to say, "Where are you going? What will I do? How come I can't go?" Mom tried to explain to Bob Dog that Dad would be back in a few days, but he didn't seem to understand.

When Mom got home that night, she realized she had inadvertently left the garage door open and Bob Dog was gone. She looked. She cried. She called for him till well after dark.

She blamed herself for forgetting to put the garage door down. She had been too distracted with Dad. It was a cold winter night and she knew how sickly Bob Dog was without the warmth of his own bed. She left the garage door up that night, hoping he'd come back. She dreaded having to tell Dad if she had lost Bob Dog. It would surely hinder his recovery as well.

Later that night, a neighbor found Bob Dog about halfway to the hospital. He had tried to track one last time. Whether he succumbed to pneumonia on that cold winter night, we don't know. But we do know that Dad loved that dog whether it had an attitude or not, and Bob Dog loved Dad whether he had an attitude or not.

My brother made the 45-minute drive to pick up Bob Dog from beside the road. He took him to his final resting place back on the family farm.

Though Bob Dog didn't make it through last winter, fortunately Dad did. Dad is not one to grieve openly, but we all knew he did. He still has yet to take on another dog.

The Preeminence
of Love

NIKI ANDERSON

---

*P*arented from prestigious stock, Oliver was the offspring of a new mix. But the Burmese kitten was a disappointment to his breeder only moments after his birth. Speckled across his shoulders were a few white hairs which disqualified him as a potential show cat. Little did the breeder know what potential lay within his "imperfect" kitten.

Dean and Cathy Anderson were at the top of the breeder's list of prospective buyers. Fortunately, they were waiting to adopt a Burmese kitten, not a show cat. The selection of a Burmese had not been without Cathy's studious comparison with other exotics. The stocky round-chested Burmese are exceptionally affectionate, the virtue that influenced Cathy's choice.

Though their new kitten would never parade before judges, he was born for a mission far more important. He would, however, receive a name that suited his fine bloodline. Because he made grand leaps accentuated by a little twist, the Andersons named him Oliver Twist. For the sake of brevity, he became Oliver.

From the beginning, Oliver loved everyone. He spread his

affection evenly among family members, leaving evidence of his loving presence with sable brown hairs (and occasionally, a disqualifying white one!) shed at the foot of each of their beds.

Just 12 months before Oliver arrived, Dean had been diagnosed with life-threatening cancer. Tests confirmed the shocking news only three days before Dean's own father died of cancer. Oliver would journey with Dean through the next six and a half years as he battled for life.

Dean began traditional treatment. But three years later, the disease had progressed, forcing him to leave his medical practice. Oliver sensed Dean's acute change in health and migrated toward him with keen sensitivity.

When radiation, chemotherapy, and experimental treatments diminished Dean's strength, two naps a day became routine. Oliver tripped upstairs to the bedroom with Dean for each session of respite. Dean would call, "Come, cat!" As the months passed, it was Oliver who summoned Dean to the stairway. He was as constant a support as the pillow under Dean's head. With golden eyes tightly closed, Oliver would slumber under Dean's upper arm.

"Oliver's companionship comforted not only Dean," said Cathy, "but I too was comforted knowing Dean was not entirely alone when I was called from his side." When years of failed drugs and procedures left Dean's body consumed by the advancing cancer cells, his attentive family and faithful kitty began living with the imminence of his passing.

Soon after his diagnosis, Dean had begun a quest to know God. He who had sailed his own boats, flown his own planes, skied, golfed, traveled, and enjoyed both professional success and a circle of extraordinary friends, sensed something fundamental was missing in his life. But his newfound relationship with God enhanced his final years and prepared him for a premature death.

In Dean's final week, his mind was troubled from large doses of pain-suppressing drugs and his fifty-eight-year-old body fought for continuing life. He mumbled in his sleep, and tossed in his bed. Oliver stayed away. The solid nine-pound cat was agitated and tense, prancing through the house, seemingly undone. But in Dean's last hours, his body relaxed, and Oliver joined him once more. When Dean passed away, Oliver was asleep, curled at his feet. Cathy, her children, and the nurse all noticed. Oliver's exemplary calm was symbolic of the peace Dean now enjoyed.

The following morning, Cathy faced the worst pain of losing her husband of twenty-two years. "I was overwhelmed with grief. I stumbled outside to the bedroom deck and unwittingly left the door ajar. Oliver followed behind. Finding no relief, I returned to the bedroom and rocked myself on the edge of the bed. I gripped my arms, helpless with hurt. Oliver, who had found a tiny pine cone on the deck, brought it inside and dropped it at my feet. He wanted to play fetch. In a perfunctory response, I threw it for him, and he brought it back. I threw it again, and heard myself chuckle. At that moment, I knew Oliver's loving ministrations would continue as we began a new life without husband and father."

And so it has been. Dean and Cathy's son, James, drops in from the nearby college to do his laundry, to check on his mom, and to get his love fix from Oliver. Marisa, their daughter, hunts for Oliver as soon as she steps through the door after school. The still youthful Oliver has become more active, but when he sleeps, he chooses the chair that now has replaced the hospital bed.

In reflections written by Dean and read at his memorial service, he referred to the words of Jesus. To Martha, Jesus said, "Only one thing is needful," meaning, the love of God. To the rich young ruler, Jesus said, "One thing you lack," again inferring, the love of God. Through his suffering Dean had come to understand what was centrally important in life—things truly needful and too often lacking—love for God and for people.

from INSPUR-R-RATIONAL STORIES FOR CAT LOVERS

ACKNOWLEDGMENTS
(continued from page ii)

"'The Loving Cat Who Kept His Word," by LeGrand Day, and "Murphy," by Alison Pfaelzer, are from *Heart Songs for Animal Lovers,* collected by Hester Mundis. Copyright © 1999 Hester Mundis. Published by Daybreak Books, an imprint of Rodale Press.

"For the Love of Snowball" and "The Revival," by Nancy B. Gibbs, are used by permission of the author.

"Nursery Duty," "Cat, a Bird's Best Friend!" and "The Preeminence of Love" are from *Inspur-r-rational Stories for Cat Lovers,* by Niki Anderson. Copyright © 1999 by Niki Anderson. Published by Honor Books.

"Memories," by Kathy Beth McDonald, is from *Dog Tales for the Heart,* edited by Sue A. Hershkowitz. Copyright © 1995. Published by High Impact Publications.

"Nobody's Bird," by Anne Watkins, is used by permission of the author.

"Each Other's Keepers," by Jaime Jacobs, is used by permission of the author.

"Restoring Rosie" is from *Love, Miracles, and Animal Healing,* by Allen M. Schoen, DVM, and Pam Proctor. Copyright © 1995 by Allen M. Schoen, D.V.M., and Pam Proctor. Published by Simon & Schuster, Inc.

"Magic" is from *Out of Harm's Way,* by Terri Crisp and Samantha Glen. Copyright © 1996 by Terri Crisp and SamAlan, Inc. Published by Pocket Books, a division of Simon & Schuster, Inc.

"Trusting Babe," by Janice Martin, is used by permission of the author.

"Side By Side," by Sissy Burggraf, is used by permission of the author.

"Mouse: The Cat Who Cared" is from *Animals Make You Feel Better,* by John G. Sutton. Copyright © 1998 by John G. Sutton. Published by Element Books, Inc.

"Look Who's Teaching Whom," by Christie Craig, is used by permission of the author.

"An Angel Named Max," by Charlene S., is from *Animal Miracles,* by Brad Steiger and Sherry Hansen Steiger. Copyright © 1999 by Brad Steiger and Sherry Hansen Steiger. Published by Adams Media Corporation.

"The First Cat," by Renie Szilak Burghardt, is used by permission of the author.

"Honey Hurricane" is from *Dogs With Jobs,* by Merrily Weisbord and Kim Kachanoff, D.V.M. Copyright © 2000 by Kim Kachanoff and Merrily Weisbord. Published by Pocket Books, a division of Simon & Schuster, Inc.

"Ode to Bob Dog," by Brenda Randolph, is used by permission of the author.

AN INVITATION TO
OUR READERS

If you would like to share a true story about an animal in your life, we invite you to send it to us. You can e-mail it to: ltta.tripod.com or mail it to LTTA, Box 214, East Greenville, PA 18041.

Some of the stories in this book came from Guideposts readers, just like you, and we welcome your participation in this inspiring series.

A Note From the Editors

This original Guideposts series was created by the Book and Inspirational Media Division of the company that publishes *Guideposts,* a monthly magazine filled with true stories of people's adventures in faith. *Guideposts* is available by subscription. All you have to do is write to Guideposts, 39 Seminary Hill Road, Carmel, New York 10512. When you subscribe, each month you can count on receiving exciting new evidence of God's presence, His guidance and His limitless love for all of us.

Guideposts is also available on the Internet by accessing our home page on the World Wide Web at www.guideposts.org. Send prayer requests to our Monday morning Prayer Fellowship. Read stories from recent issues of our magazines, *Guideposts, Angels on Earth, Clarity, Guideposts for Kids* and *Guideposts for Teens,* and follow our popular book of daily devotionals, *Daily Guideposts.* Excerpts from some of our best-selling books are also available.